An OPUS book

Medieval Writers and Their Work

J. A. Burrow

Medieval Writers and Their Work

Middle English Literature and its Background 1100–1500

Oxford   New York

OXFORD UNIVERSITY PRESS

Oxford University Press, Walton Street, Oxford OX2 6DP

Oxford New York Toronto
Delhi Bombay Calcutta Madras Karachi
Petaling Jaya Singapore Hong Kong Tokyo
Nairobi Dar es Salaam Cape Town
Melbourne Auckland

and associated companies in
Berlin Ibadan

Oxford is a trade mark of Oxford University Press

First published 1982 as an Oxford University Press paperback
and simultaneously in a hardback edition
Reprinted 1983, 1987, 1989

British Library Cataloguing in Publication Data
Burrow, J. A.
Medieval writers and their work: an introduction
to Middle English literature.
1. English literature—Middle English, 1100–1500 History and criticism.
I. Title
820'.9'001   PR281
ISBN 0–19–289122–7

Library of Congress Cataloging in Publication Data
Burrow, J. A. (John Anthony)
Medieval writers and their work. (OPUS)
Bibliography: p.
Includes index.
1. English literature—Middle English, 1100–1500—History and criticism.
2. England—Civilization—Medieval period, 1066–1485.
I. Title. II. Series
PR255.B8   820'.9'001   81–16967
ISBN 0–19–289122–7

Printed in Great Britain by
The Guernsey Press Co. Ltd.,
Guernsey, Channel Islands

Preface

This book offers neither a history nor a survey of Middle English literature: a survey may be found in Kemp Malone and A. C. Baugh, *The Middle
Ages* (2nd edn., 1967), and Derek Pearsall provides a history of the verse in
Old English and Middle English Poetry (1977). The present book is designed as an introduction. At the risk of giving an exaggerated impression
of the strangeness of Middle English writings, I have concentrated on
some of the chief differences which confront a reader of modern literature
when he first approaches them: differences in the notion of literature itself
(Chapter 1), in the circumstances under which writings were produced
and received (Chapter 2), in the types of writing produced (Chapter 3), and
in the kinds of meaning to be found in them (Chapter 4). Chapters 1 and 5
also attempt to characterize the Middle English period in relation to earlier
and later periods of English literature.

Texts are quoted from the editions cited in the Bibliography. Bible
quotations are from the Authorized Version. Translations of Dante's
Divine Comedy are taken from the version by C. H. Sisson (1980).

I would like to thank Stephen Medcalf, Alastair Minnis, Charles
Runacres, John Scattergood, Thorlac Turville-Petre, and many students
and colleagues for giving me ideas and advice.

The book is dedicated to the memory of F. W. Bateson.

J. A. B.

Contents

1 The period and the literature

The phrase 'Middle English' has an academic and somewhat unidiomatic flavour. It was first coined to designate a period in the history of the English language. Historical philologists in the nineteenth century, most of them German, liked to see in the history of a language three phases: Old (*alt-*), Middle (*mittel-*), and New or Modern (*neu-*). This triadic scheme fitted the history of English quite well. Old English could only be the language of pre-Conquest, Anglo-Saxon England. New English presumably extended back from the present day to the beginning of modern times—say, the first Tudors. In between lay Middle English. This was distinguished from Old English chiefly by a simplified system of inflexion and a vocabulary enriched from French and Scandinavian sources, and from Modern English by inflexions still further simplified and a vocabulary further enriched and diversified, especially from Latin. On the strength of changes such as these, philologists fixed the beginnings of Middle English in the period 1100–1150 and its end around 1450–1500.[1]

Philology and literary history being twin disciplines, it is not surprising that literary historians were quick to adopt the concept of 'Middle English'. The three or four hundred years in question soon came to be seen also as a literary period. It seemed natural to consider the works surviving from these centuries—*Ancrene Wisse* and *The Owl and the Nightingale*, *Sir Gawain and the Green Knight* and *The Cloud of Unknowing*, the *Canterbury Tales* and *Morte d'Arthur*—as representatives not only of a stage in the English language, but also of a stage in the development of English literature. Yet this usage cannot be accepted without question, even in a book such as this, committed by its title to the concept of Middle English Literature. Literary historians are accustomed to borrow like jackdaws from other disciplines when it comes to defining and naming periods. They use, for instance, the reigns of kings and queens: 'Jacobean drama', 'Victorian poetry'. The status of such borrowed labels must always be questionable, even when they are borrowed, as in the case of 'Middle English', from a discipline more closely related to literary studies than is political history. Language is the medium of literature, and the state of the language at any given time can hardly fail to carry literary consequences.

However, the particular features which interest philologists and form the basis of their periodizations (inflexions, for instance) are not always fraught with profound literary implications. So there is no necessary reason for the literary historian or critic to pay any attention at all to linguistic periods, any more than to kings' reigns.

Yet the philologists' concept of Middle English has in fact proved useful for literary purposes; and this utility is not merely a matter of happy accident, as a glance at some of the linguistic changes marking the beginning of the period will suggest. The main changes in vocabulary and inflexion can be seen by comparing two passages from the *Peterborough Chronicle*—a version of the *Anglo-Saxon Chronicle* which the monks of Peterborough kept up until the middle of the twelfth century. The monks' entries for the years up to 1121 are written in passable Old English. Thus one of them writes as follows about William the Conqueror, on the occasion of his death in 1087:

> Se cyng Willelm þe we embe sprecað wæs swiðe wis man, and swiðe rice, and wurðfulre and strengere þonne ænig his foregenga wære. He wæs milde þam godum mannum þe God lufedon, and ofer eall gemett stearc þam mannum þe wiðcwædon his willan.

> King William, of whom we speak, was a very wise man, and very powerful, more distinguished and more powerful than any of his predecessors were. He was gentle with those good men who loved God, and beyond measure severe with those men who opposed his will.

All the words here are native Anglo-Saxon words; and the inflexions (except in *wurðfulre* and *strengere*, which have *-e* for *-a*) conform to the usage of standard Old English : *-að* for the present plural indicative of verbs (*sprecað*), *-on* for the preterite plural indicative (*lufedon*, *wiðcwædon*), *-um* for the dative plural of nouns and adjectives (*godum mannum*). The last Peterborough chronicler, by contrast, writing about seventy years later, speaks as follows of the anarchy in the reign of King Stephen:

> Ævric rice man his castles makede and agænes him heolden; and fylden þe land ful of castles. Hi swencten swyðe þe wrecce men of þe land mid castelweorces.

> Every great man built his own castles and held them against him [the king]; and they filled the land full of castles. They sorely burdened the wretched men of the land with working on the castles.

Here preterite plural *-on* appears as *-en* (*heolden*, *fylden*, *swencten*), a spelling which represents the vowel heard in the unstressed syllable of a modern word such as *London*. The phrase *men of the land*, so natural to us, in fact illustrates a number of new developments from Old English: a new, indeclinable definite article *the*, a noun undeclined after a preposition (*of* takes the dative in Old English), and also the substitution of a prepositional phrase for a declined noun. *Castles* is a loan word from French, very characteristic of the new age.

It is by no means obvious why changes such as these in the written language should provide a suitable terminus for a literary period. Yet they can in fact be seen as symptomatic of far-reaching and profound changes in English culture in the century after the Norman Conquest. As it happens, the simplification of the inflexional system is not in itself such a symptom. Philologists believe that this development had already been going on for centuries in the spoken language, partly because of a general blurring of vowel quality in unstressed syllables. What is significant is the breakdown of a tradition which had taught scribes to observe distinctions in writing which they did not observe in speech. The Peterborough monk who wrote about William probably pronounced his preterite plural endings in just the same way as did his successor who wrote about Stephen (as in Modern *London*); but he had been taught to write *-on* here, reserving *-en* for other parts of the verb conjugation. He was still faithful to a scribal tradition definitively established in the tenth century at Winchester, the ancient capital of the kingdom of Wessex; and what he wrote was, in all essentials, still the standard literary language, now known as Late West Saxon, which prevailed at the time of the Conquest. This Standard Old English showed considerable powers of survival after the Conquest; but its eventual collapse, traceable in the *Peterborough Chronicle*, was inevitable. It had derived its strength and authority, as standard languages generally do, from the military, economic, and political dominance of the area in which it originated—in this case, Wessex, whose kings had reconquered the Danelaw and become the first kings of all England. After the Conquest, Wessex became no more than a province of Norman England, and Winchester dwindled into a provincial centre. So a Winchester Standard became an anachronism.

The eventual disintegration of the old standard written language should not be taken to mark the end of all Anglo-Saxon literary traditions. Indeed, both the traditions most vigorously represented in manuscripts of the late Old English period survived well into the period of Middle English. The remarkable school of Anglo-Saxon prose writers, of whom the best known are Ælfric (*c*. 955–1020) and Wulfstan (d. 1023), found successors two hundred years later in the authors of *Ancrene Wisse* and the homilies of the Katherine Group; and Anglo-Saxon alliterative poetry is still vigorously alive in Laȝamon's *Brut*, a verse chronicle of the kings of Britain composed, like *Ancrene Wisse*, in the early thirteenth century. Yet it is significant that these two cardinal works both come from the remote West Midlands—Laȝamon's *Brut* from the banks of the Severn, *Ancrene Wisse* probably from the region of Lingen in the depths of Herefordshire. Anglo-Saxon traditions survived; but they no longer occupied in 1200 the central position which they had in 1000. They now belonged more to the marches than to the capital. The native literary culture, in fact, was receding during the twelfth century; and the linguistic changes associated with the collapse of the old written standard are symptoms of that recession.

At the same time, other distinctive features of Early Middle English point towards that new literary culture which was to occupy a capital position throughout the Middle English period—the Francophone culture which extended, after the Conquest, to England. After 1066, England came to form, with Normandy, a single 'Channel kingdom'; and the vernacular spoken in this kingdom by the rich and powerful was not English (West Saxon or otherwise), but French. The relative status of the two vernaculars may be suggested by the fact that, whereas Laȝamon apparently wrote his English *Brut* for an obscure audience in Worcestershire, his French source, the *Brut* of the Anglo-Norman poet Wace, was presented by its author to Eleanor of Aquitaine, the great cosmopolitan lady who married King Henry II of England.

Some of the features by which philologists distinguish Middle from Old English testify directly to the dominance of French in the England of the Norman and Angevin kings. The presence of the French word *castle* in the language of the last Peterborough chronicler has little literary significance in itself; but it is a symptom of new circumstances which themselves are of fundamental importance. The vernacular culture of Anglo-Saxon England had its roots in the world of Germania. The tradition of alliterative verse, in particular, goes back to common Germanic origins, being shared by other Germanic peoples such as those of Iceland and Germany. The new vernacular culture of twelfth-century England, on the other hand, belonged not to Germania but to Romania. Much Romance poetry, indeed, was composed for Anglo-Norman patrons, in dialects of Anglo-Norman, Norman, or French.[2] Wace, who came from Jersey, presented his *Brut* to the queen of England; two early French versions of the Tristram story, the *Tristans* of Thomas and Béroul, were both probably composed for audiences in England; and it is likely that Marie de France wrote her *Lais* in England. Much of this Francophone literary activity centred, it would appear, in the court of King Henry II of England— himself, of course, a French-speaker.

The twelfth century is a complex and bewildering age, in which the distribution of kingdoms and languages and literatures does not at all coincide with the boundaries familiar to us. In that period—as today, but for exactly opposite reasons—the two categories of literature in English and literature in England quite fail to coincide. Whereas today literature in England is only a part of literature in English, in the twelfth century literature in English was only a part—and very much a subordinate part— of literature in England. Yet it is still possible for a student of English literature (literature in English) to get some idea of the Romance culture which prevailed at that time, if only by registering its influence upon English writings. This influence can be seen, for instance, in *The Owl and the Nightingale*, a poem composed in southern English perhaps about 1200. Like his contemporary Laȝamon, this writer was acquainted with the French poetry of the court of Henry II; but, unlike Laȝamon, he adopts the manner and metre, as well as the matter, of that poetry. Whereas the *Brut* employs a version of the old alliterative line, *The Owl and the Nightingale* employs the sprightly octosyllabic couplet made fashionable by writers such as Marie de France (whose work the author certainly knew) and Chrétien de Troyes. It also catches something of their lightness of touch. Here, for instance, the Nightingale is claiming that her song teaches useful moral lessons to young girls:

> That maide wot, hwanne ich swike,
> That luve is mine songes iliche:
> For hit nis bute a lutel breth
> That sone kumeth & sone geth.
> That child bi me hit understond,
> An his unred to red wend,
> An iseith wel bi mine songe
> That dusi luve ne last noght longe.   (1459–66)

That girl realizes, when I stop singing, that love is like my songs: for it is nothing but a little breath, that soon comes and soon goes. The child understands that from me, and turns all her foolishness into good sense, and sees well from my singing that foolish love does not last long.

Despite his frequent references to King Alfred as a source of proverbial wisdom, this poet seems to owe very little to Anglo-Saxon traditions. *The Owl and the Nightingale* belongs to a world quite different from that of a late Old English poem such as *The Battle of Maldon*.

So it is more than a coincidence that the philologists' division of Middle from Old English round about 1100–1150 should have proved valid also for students of literature: the recession of Anglo-Saxon culture and the ascendancy of French led, three or four generations after the Norman Conquest, to the kinds of fundamental change associated with a new period, as well in literature as in language. To see how these changes serve, not only to define the beginning of the Middle English period, but also to establish the character of the period as a whole, it will be necessary now to set them in a broader European context.

The expression 'Middle Ages' ('Medium Aevum') was originally coined by Renaissance humanists to denote the whole period which lay between the fall of classical civilization and the establishment of modern civilization in their own day. They had no difficulty in characterizing this huge period: it was an age of barbarism. Barbarism, for these scholars and artists, meant ignorance of those canons of taste which the Greeks and Romans had established in antiquity and which they themselves had rediscovered in modern times. With the decline of classical taste and training in the twentieth century, this vigorously polemical characterization has lost some of its force; and no clear and commanding new characterization has arisen to take its place. Indeed, modern scholarship has disclosed so much change and variety within the thousand years from 500 to 1500 that the old, broad, humanistic conception of the Middle Ages seems to have lost its utility—for the time being, at least. In its place, we now most often have a less sweeping periodization, which splits the old, broad period into two. The division is customarily put somewhere about the year 1100, in the century 1050–1150. The old term 'Dark Ages' may be used of the first of these periods, while the second tends nowadays to monopolize the title of 'Middle Ages'.

This current use of the terms Middle Ages and Medieval in their narrower sense, to refer to a period of some four hundred years starting about 1100, raises certain difficulties. Quite apart from the risk of confusion with the older, broader usage, it is no longer possible to say what these Middle Ages are in the middle between. Yet some kind of division round about 1100 seems indispensable. Between the early eleventh century and the late twelfth century, West Europe seems to have undergone, in almost all departments of life, a transformation.[3] Political conditions became more stable. Trade and agriculture boomed. The population began to increase. Town life revived and the bourgeoisie became a power in the land. Warriors began to see themselves as knights and to display the heraldic trappings of chivalry. In the courts of the great, ladies demanded new refinements of courtesy, especially from their admirers ('courtly love'). In all the arts, new forms were developed to meet the age's luxuriant taste for grace and complexity. Gothic architecture supersedes the sturdy Romanesque, romances of chivalry take the place of the old heroic narratives, music develops towards polyphony. In religion, the founding of new orders, such as the Cistercians, is associated with a new religious sensibility, which finds its most characteristic expression in the cult of the Virgin

Mary. There is a revival of interest in classical Antiquity, such that modern scholars can even speak of a Twelfth-Century Renaissance.[4] Learned disciplines, largely confined in the previous age to the monastic schools, enter a new, dynamic phase, first in cathedral schools (Chartres) and later in the new universities (Paris, Oxford). As the Mediterranean Sea becomes open once more to the peoples of Europe (this is the age of the First Crusade), Western scholars rediscover, chiefly through Muslim intermediaries, much of ancient Greek science and philosophy. This was the beginning of the age of Aristotle, and scholasticism was to prove its most characteristic intellectual achievement.

Middle English literature occupies a rather modest place in this brave new world, as beneficiary rather than as contributor. English was at this time an insular language which few foreigners could speak or understand; and our writings seem to have excited little curiosity abroad. The first English text of any sort known to have been translated for foreign readers is John Gower's *Confessio Amantis*, translated shortly after its composition into Portuguese by an English canon of Lisbon and subsequently into Castilian; but this is itself an isolated case, reflecting a special relationship between England and the Iberian peninsula in the fourteenth century. Even Gower's great contemporary and friend, Geoffrey Chaucer, remained almost unknown abroad. It is true that a contemporary French poet, Eustache Deschamps, composed a ballade in his praise; but he speaks of Chaucer (conventional generalities apart) only as a 'great translator', referring to the English poet's translation of the French *Roman de la Rose*.

The French have not always been generous, perhaps, in their appreciation of English writers; but Deschamps's description of Chaucer as a 'grant translateur', partial though it is, points to a cardinal truth about Middle English literature as a whole: its heavy dependence upon French. The indebtedness of Early Middle English writers such as Laȝamon to French writers such as Wace might be put down to the particular political circumstances of the time; but the Norman Conquest, although it certainly played a large part in shifting the orbit of English literature from Germania to Romania, cannot serve as an explanation for the priority and dominance of French literature throughout the whole Middle English period. After the loss of Normandy by King John in 1204, England no longer formed part of a Channel kingdom; yet even in the age of Chaucer and Gower, nearly two hundred years later, French influence was still dominant. Richard II still possessed some French territories, but he was not, like Henry II, a continental monarch; and, although the French chronicler and poet, Froissart, reports that he spoke French well, Richard's mother tongue was probably English. He was, indeed, essentially an English king. Yet English writers of the Ricardian period can still be regarded, not without justice, as 'great translators' from the French.

The truth is that English literature would certainly have entered the French orbit even if William had not killed Harold at Hastings; for it is one of the most striking features of the European Middle Ages (after about 1100) that France dominates almost all departments of cultural and intellectual life. The great creative activity of the eleventh and twelfth centuries had its main centres in France, especially in the valleys of the Loire and the Seine. Gothic architecture established itself at the Abbey of Saint-Denis, just north of Paris, and in the Cathedral of Chartres, just as scholasticism established itself at the newly founded University of Paris. The great new order of monks, the Cistercians, took its name from Cîteaux in Burgundy and was established by a Frenchman, St Bernard. In vernacular literature, the first and in some ways the greatest of Arthurian romances come from the pen of Chrétien de Troyes (in Champagne): versions already subtle and sophisticated of the adventures of Lancelot, Perceval, Ywain, and other Knights of the Round Table. These French romances were imitated and translated, not just in England, but in remote Iceland. They also exerted a decisive influence in the great age of medieval German poetry, on the *Parzival* of Wolfram von Eschenbach and the *Tristan* of Gottfried von Strassburg. Chrétien has every justification for claiming, in a passage of *Cligès* (31–6), that the centre of civilization, after moving west from Greece to Rome, now rested in France: 'Greece had the first renown in chivalry and in learning. Then chivalry came to Rome, and the heyday of learning, which has now come into France. God grant that it may be maintained there!'

French influence is therefore not a peculiar mark of conquered England, but a general characteristic of medieval Europe; and it persisted in England, as elsewhere, to the end of the period. In Middle English literature the evidences for this influence are everywhere to be seen. English romance, for instance, is heavily dependent upon French. Rather surprisingly, only one Middle English version from Chrétien de Troyes survives (*Ywain and Gawain*, adapted from Chrétien's *Yvain*), although it is clear that his unfinished romance of Perceval, with its various lengthy continuations by other hands, circulated widely in the north of England. Its influence can be seen in *Sir Gawain and the Green Knight*. French verse romances frequently provided models for the English metrical romances, some of which attempted to imitate the fluent octosyllabic couplet perfected by Chrétien and his successors for purposes of narrative. The species of French romance known as Breton lay, created by Marie de France in the twelfth century, attracted considerable imitation in English. *Sir Lanval* is a translation of one of Marie's lays; and *Sir Orfeo* treats the story of Orpheus and Eurydice in her manner.

Perhaps the most striking instance of the dependence of Middle English romancers upon French models is Sir Thomas Malory's *Morte d'Arthur*. The fashion for verse romance in the France of Chrétien de Troyes had been followed there, in the thirteenth century, by a precocious cultivation of narrative in prose, whose chief monument is the so-called Vulgate Cycle of prose romances. This huge sequence of Arthurian stories achieves something of that authoritative and orderly completeness so much prized in the thirteenth century, the great age of the Summa, and it became a standard text. When Dante, in his *De Vulgari Eloquentia*, speaks of 'Arturi regis ambages pulcerrime' ('the exquisitely intricate adventures of King Arthur'), he was probably thinking of this cycle, with its elaborate inter-lacing of stories; and certainly it was the Vulgate *Lancelot* which he imagined his Paolo and Francesca reading together on the occasion of their first embrace (*Inferno* V). In England the Vulgate romances appear to have enjoyed a similar currency; and the most sophisticated of the English romancers, the author of *Sir Gawain and the Green Knight*, draws on them for many details of his Arthurian world. But it is evidence of a certain cultural time-lag between France and England that English writers did not at first share their continental contemporaries' modern taste for narrative unencumbered by rhyme. Just as the verse romances of Chrétien were not matched in England until two centuries later, in the age of Chaucer, Gower, and the *Gawain*-poet, so the prose romances of the Vulgate Cycle were not matched until the time of Malory (d. 1471). Large parts of the *Morte d'Arthur* are in fact directly translated or adapted from Vulgate romances. Malory's version of the Grail story, for instance, is based on the Vulgate *Queste del Saint Graal*; and the Vulgate *Mort Artu* furnished much of his tragic last book. Apparently, too, it was from the Vulgate compilers that Malory derived the ambition to record, not just a single adventure or string of adventures, but the whole history of Arthur and the Knights of the Round Table.

Romance, in prose or verse, is the most distinctive product of the vernacular literatures of the Middle Ages—so much so that this is often characterized as the Age of Romance, as against an earlier Age of Epic.[5] But the distinctive Frenchness of Middle English literature is not confined to that dominant genre. Indeed, in the fourteenth and fifteenth centuries English poetry came to owe less to the romances than to the allegorical and lyrical poetry of France.

The rise of allegorical poetry in France in the thirteenth century had more or less coincided with the decline of verse romance there. Courtly allegory seems to have provided polite audiences with a new and more congenial kind of narrative poetry. Since prose was taking over the busi-ness of chronicling the knightly adventures of romance heroes (feats of arms which had perhaps never in any case appealed much to the ladies who formed such an important part of the audience of courtly romance), poets were increasingly left free to exploit the rich seams of psychology and sentiment already present in the works of Chrétien de Troyes, Marie de France, and their followers. The decisive step was taken by Guillaume de Lorris in his *Roman de la Rose*. This unfinished poem, completed some forty years later by Jean de Meun and partly translated by Chaucer in the following century, established a new kind of vernacular narrative poem representing, in the form of a dream or vision, an allegorical or symbolical world in which the persons and events typically shadow forth aspects of the experience of love. The very name of the poem, 'Roman *de la Rose*', throws down a challenge to the older poetry of wars and heroes, for it assumes a sophisticated disregard for big things and violent events: this romance is about a *rose*. The audience capable of appreciating such delicate chamber poetry existed in thirteenth-century England too; but it was still at that time a French-speaking audience, and would have been satisfied by the *Roman de la Rose* itself and its many French imitators. It was only a century later, when polite circles in England had turned to English, that poets began to produce English poems adapted to these refined tastes. Gower's *Confessio Amantis*, the *Gawain*-poet's *Pearl*, Chaucer's *Book of the Duchess* and *Parliament of Fowls*, Clanvowe's *Book of Cupid*—all these poems testify, in the age of Richard II, to the continuing creative influence of the *Roman de la Rose*. The same influence can be seen in the next generation, in Lydgate's *Temple of Glas* or in the *Kingis Quair* of King James I of Scotland. Indeed, the tradition of dream-allegory survived to the very end of the Middle Ages: Dunbar and Gavin Douglas in Scotland, and even Skelton in the England of Henry VIII, all wrote poems recognizably descended from Guillaume de Lorris's seminal work.

The history of the secular lyric in the earlier part of the Middle English period is obscure, largely because so few texts survive from before 1300; but it seems clear that here too, in the fourteenth and fifteenth centuries at least, France led the way. In the work of French poets such as Guillaume de Machaut, indeed, the traditions of love lyric and courtly allegory are almost inseparable. Machaut will insert lyrics into his allegorical narratives, just as Chaucer does in the *Prologue to the Legend of Good Women*. So the same English poets who write dream allegories in the courtly French manner also frequently imitate the 'grand chant courtois' of France. Chaucer's ballades and roundels belong to this tradition, as do the ballades of his disciple Hoccleve. In the fifteenth century, this kind of lyric became increasingly elaborate and, eventually, sclerotic, both in France and in England, under the influence of the Burgundian school of rhetorical poetry; but William Dunbar's lyrics composed about 1500 in the elaborate

Burgundian manner, sometimes called 'aureate', show what the 'grand chant courtois' was still capable of, even in the last years of the Middle Ages.

Romances in verse and prose, allegories of love, and courtly lyrics were by no means the only genres of French writing to attract English imitators. The French *fabliau* provided Chaucer with his model for such Canterbury Tales as those of the Miller, the Reeve, and the Shipman; and his contemporary, William Langland, drew largely in his *Piers Plowman* upon a French tradition of religious allegorical poetry whose chief master was Guillaume de Deguileville. Not that French was the only literature to influence English writers at this time. Apart from the Italian influence upon Chaucer, it would seem that other European vernaculars hardly enter into the picture; but Latin literature, both classical and medieval, had an importance for the better-educated writers of the period which not even French could equal. Chaucer's debt to Ovid, for instance, exceeds even his debt to the *Roman de la Rose*. But this dominance of Latin literature is not, like the dominance of French, a *distinctive* feature of the Middle English period. Latin was already important for Old English literature, as modern scholarship has increasingly demonstrated; and it continued to be important, of course, in the Renaissance period. By contrast, the dominance of French literature began, as we have seen, just at the beginning of the Middle English period. And the decline of that influence roughly coincided, we may now add, with the end of the period.

It would not be possible to provide precise dates here. Philologists customarily give the dates 1450 or 1500 for the end of the Middle English period of the language; but it can hardly be said that the lexical, morphological, and phonological changes which distinguish Shakespeare's English from Chaucer's reached a critical point at either date, even allowing the customary latitude to round figures. In any case, even if philology could offer a date, literary history would have little use for it. I shall return to this matter in the last chapter; but for the moment it may be asserted that there is no sharp break perceptible between medieval and Renaissance. Poets such as Wyatt, Spenser, and George Herbert derive far more than their continental contemporaries from the medieval past. There were profound changes, of course, but these occurred gradually. Thus, a poet such as Skelton, writing in the time of the first Tudors, Henry VII and Henry VIII, might count as a medieval poet on some criteria and a Renaissance poet on others. However, not all criteria are equally important; and the decline of French as a paramount influence is a more useful criterion than most. It is a sound instinct which has led literary historians to attach special importance to the Italian influence upon Wyatt and Surrey, as a sign of the new age.

II

Many writers on medieval literature in the last thirty years or so have defined their approach specifically as critical, rather than philological or antiquarian. The watchword for this approach has been to 'study literature as literature'. The tautologous form of the slogan has the effect of claiming for the literary approach, where literature is concerned, priority and privilege. But not all the many texts surviving from the Middle English period, obviously, can count as literature. The question of which do count, and on what criteria, has been generally avoided, perhaps because it seems pedantic; but it raises, as I shall hope to show in this section, some far-reaching issues. The concept of Middle English *literature* is, in fact, a problematic and challenging one.

One should not expect texts in any period to fall into two clearly defined categories, literary and non-literary. The complexity of texts and the complexity of the notion of literature itself are such that borderline cases will always arise—texts which meet some criteria of literature but not others, and texts which meet those criteria in some parts but not in others. Nevertheless, modern criticism has arrived at a notion of literature which, when applied to modern texts, yields fairly definite results. For practical purposes of library classification, university syllabus-making, and the like, it is generally agreed that literature has three main branches: poetry, prose fiction, and drama. Because 'literature' is an honorific term with strong evaluative implications, not all texts of these three sorts will be admitted, some being excluded as sub-literary; but otherwise one can safely say that poems, prose fictions, and plays together form the triple core of the current working notion of literature. In practice, too, the history of English literature since the Middle Ages largely resolves itself into histories of these three types of writing, each of which presents to the historian a quite well-formed and continuous tradition. By contrast, the huge and miscellaneous corpus of non-fictional prose (treatises, histories, letters, sermons) attracts relatively little attention either from critics or from literary historians, except in so far as it assists the study of poems, novels, and plays. In this respect, indeed, the notion of literature seems to have become more and more exclusive in recent years, with literary readers tending to leave Clarendon to the historians, Bacon to the historians of science, Berkeley to the philosophers, and so on.

To understand why this modern working notion of literature applies so imperfectly to medieval texts, we must glance briefly at its foundations. What are the presuppositions of the familiar equation: Literature = Poetry + Prose Fiction + Drama? What criteria does it imply? There is no simple answer to this question. Some have attempted to define literature in terms of the mental faculty which produces it (imagination, usually) or in terms of some characteristic subject matter (feelings, most often); but the most promising definitions are of a more formal kind. Of these, two main varieties predominate in current discussions. The first seeks the main criterion of literariness, or *littérarité*, in the way literary texts use language. Literature exploits potentialities in language which non-literary discourse neglects. It works language itself into an object of aesthetic contemplation. Roman Jakobson, the Russian linguist and Formalist, states a view of this sort in his bald definition of the 'poetic function' of language: 'The distinctive feature of poetry lies in the fact that a word is perceived as a word and not merely a proxy for the denoted object or an outburst of an emotion, that words and their arrangement, their meaning, their outward and inward form acquire weight and value of their own'.[6]

The other kind of formal criterion also concerns the relation between literary and non-literary discourse; but here the difference is sought in the kinds of truth considered proper to each. Literature is distinguished from history or philosophy or science as a fictional, or non-affirmative, or non-pragmatic, or hypothetical mode of discourse. It is not committed, in any ordinary, straightforward fashion, to the truth of the events which it reports or the ideas which it propounds. It does not 'propose truth for its *immediate* object', as Coleridge says in *Biographia Literaria*. Northrop Frye says: 'In literature the standards of outward meaning are secondary, for literary works do not pretend to describe or assert, and hence are not true, not false, and yet not tautological either'.[7] The philosopher J. L. Austin puts the point dryly: 'Walt Whitman does not *seriously* incite the eagle of liberty to soar'.

These two kinds of criterion are not mutually exclusive. On the contrary, they combine very readily in most modern thinking about literature. When the French critic Gérard Genette defines literature as 'un message qui tend partiellement à se résorber en spectacle' ('a form of communication which tends in part to convert itself into an object of contemplation'), he implies both the fictionality of literature and the 'poetic function' of its discourse.[8] The language of literature may be said to tend 'partiellement à se résorber en spectacle', but so too can the ideas which it propounds and the events which it reports. The two processes appear, in a formula such as Genette's, to be manifestations of a single deeper process. Genette is here entirely typical of modern thinking. Two kinds of criterion combine in a single complex idea of *littérarité*.

Nothing very like this idea of literature appears to have occurred to medieval thinkers. The idea of a 'poetic function' of language was familiar to grammarians and rhetoricians under a different name: 'eloquence'.

When Jakobson describes how 'words and their arrangement, their meaning, their outward and inward form acquire weight and value of their own', he aligns himself with an ancient tradition of thinking about eloquent speech, inherited by medieval schoolmen from the rhetoricians of antiquity. However, these rhetorical criteria were only rarely associated, either in antiquity or in the Middle Ages, with criteria of my second sort. It is not that medieval people were unconcerned with the distinction between fiction and fact; but that distinction appears to have played a relatively modest part in their typology of texts. More than any other text, perhaps, it was Aristotle's *Poetics* which taught the West to regard fictionality (implied in Aristotle's doctrine of imitation) as a prime characteristic of poetry; but medieval Europe had access to the *Poetics* only through a Latin translation made (about 1256) from an Arab commentary.[9] This version suppressed and distorted Aristotle's notion of imitation, substituting for it the idea that poetry's chief function was to praise virtue and blame vice. That conception of poetry as a branch of ethics is characteristic of the Middle Ages; but, whatever its merits, it provided no incentive to distinguish literary from non-literary texts. That incentive came in the sixteenth century, with the full rediscovery of Aristotle's thought on the matter. It was only then that the criterion of fictionality assumed prime importance in post-classical literary theory, first in the writings of the Italian humanists. The classic statement by an English humanist is that of Sir Philip Sidney, in his *Apology for Poetry* (1595): 'Now for the poet, he nothing affirms, and therefore never lieth. For, as I take it, to lie is to affirm that to be true which is false; so as the other artists [men of learning], and especially the historians, affirming many things, can, in the cloudy knowledge of mankind, hardly escape from many lies. But the poet (as I said before) never affirmeth'.[10] The same idea lies behind Ben Jonson's blunt comment on Du Bartas, author of an epic poem on the creation of the world, that he was 'not a poet but a verser, because he wrote not fiction'.[11] Both authors perhaps had in mind the dictum in Aristotle's *Poetics*: 'You might put the work of Herodotus into verse, and it would still be a species of history [i.e. not poetry]'.

The old rhetorical criteria were not superseded by these new, humanistic criteria based on Aristotle's concept of imitation: on the contrary, as I have suggested, our idea of literature may be regarded as a product of their combination. The medieval concept of eloquent discourse is therefore not in itself unfamiliar to the modern reader. But where, as in much medieval 'literary criticism', rhetorical criteria operate in isolation, without reference to considerations of fictivity, the results will now often seem very queer. Consider what Chaucer's Host says, in the *Canterbury Tales*, when calling on the Clerk for a story:

'Telle us som murie thyng of aventures.
Youre termes, youre colours, and youre figures,
Keepe hem in stoor til so be that ye endite
Heigh style, as whan that men to kynges write.'

(IV 15–18)

Keepe hem in stoor] store them away   *endite*] compose

The shock is in the last line. The Host's characterization of high style as a matter of special diction ('termes') and rhetorical devices ('colours' and 'figures') may suggest a 'rhetorical concept of literature'; but his suggestion of a suitable occasion on which to use it forces us, in its uncompromising strangeness, to realize that he is not thinking in terms of 'literature' at all—unless that label can be attached to a category of texts which includes the correspondence of the royal chancelleries.

There exist many medieval Latin treatises—grammars, rhetorics, and arts of poetry—which deal with 'terms' and 'colours' and 'figures' and other features of eloquent discourse; but these, too, display a typology of texts in which our category of literature makes no appearance. In his *Parisiana Poetria*, composed about 1220, the English rhetorician John of Garland declares his intention of teaching *ars eloquentiae*, 'the art of eloquence', dividing his matter into three parts: *ars dictandi*, *ars metricandi*, and *ars rithmicandi*.[12] The two last terms distinguish the two main types of medieval Latin verse: quantitative verse in the classical manner ('metric') and rhymed syllabic verse in the modern manner ('rhythmic'). As its title suggests, much of John's treatise does indeed concern itself with poetry; but John also discusses prose; and it is that discussion which shows how far he is from any notion of literature. His concern is with eloquent prose, but that for him is chiefly a matter of formal letter writing. This is what *ars dictandi* chiefly teaches: 'heigh style, as whan that men to kynges write'. Like Chaucer's Host, in fact, John recognizes no frontier between literature and letters. The art of eloquence is no more relevant to poems than it is to formal correspondence—or to deeds, or indentures, or summonses, or sermons.

Given this category of eloquent discourse, overriding distinctions which seem fundamental to us, it is no surprise to find that the distinction between fictive and non-fictive occupies a low and obscure place in John of Garland's scheme, occurring in a digression on kinds of narration, in the course of a chapter devoted to common vices of prose and verse (Chapter V). John distinguishes three types of narrative: *fabula*, which concerns 'events that are untrue, and do not pretend to be true'; *hystoria*, which 'reports an event which has taken place [*res gesta*] long before the memory of our age'; and *argumentum*, which concerns 'a fictitious event [*res ficta*] which nevertheless could have happened, as is the case in comedies'. This triple distinction, which goes back at least as far as Cicero (*De Inventione* I 19), has considerable interest in its own right. The definition of *argumentum* gives the lie to those who suggest that the notion of realistic fiction was not available to medieval readers and writers. However, the present point is to note how little importance John attaches to the distinction between *res gesta* and *res ficta*. It occurs tardily, in a digression, as a subdivision of a subdivision. Unlike Ben Jonson, John of Garland seems little concerned whether a poet or other kind of eloquent writer 'writes fiction' or not. His interest lies elsewhere, in *ars eloquentiae* itself.

It would be quite wrong to suggest that all medieval 'literary criticism' (the phrase cannot be used without reserve) belongs to the rhetorical tradition represented by John of Garland. Twelfth-century France and fourteenth-century Italy, in particular, furnish evidence of a loftier view of the poet—something like the humanists' Neoplatonic view of the poet as an inspired seer, expressing profound truths in his fables.[13] In so far as this tradition claims that the truths so expressed in poetry cannot be translated into any other kind of discourse, it perhaps approaches modern notions of a special literary kind of truth; but in practice even Neoplatonic criticism in the Middle Ages tended to decode poetic allegories into plain statements of moral, cosmological, or historical truth—statements which were not themselves in any sense fictive. Nor can it be claimed, in any case, that the work of Middle English poets, with the possible exception of Chaucer, invites discussion in Neoplatonic terms. The more mundane tradition represented by John of Garland seems, whether we like it or not, more generally relevant.

The reader of Middle English literature, then, has to recognize that his authors would not normally have thought of their works as representing any special or privileged literary mode of discourse. It does not follow from this conclusion, of course, that the notion of literature cannot be used in the study of such old texts. Criticism is not confined to concepts available to authors; and in so far as the ideas of contemporary theorists such as John of Garland merely reflect an undeveloped literary theory, lacking even a knowledge of Aristotle's *Poetics*, they are best neglected. But some of those ideas faithfully reflect, in their very peculiarities, a real state of affairs different from what we are accustomed to. Thus, John of Garland's classification of eloquent texts, as we have seen, makes no important distinction between fictive and non-fictive discourse. Eloquence, for him, does not entail fictivity, as it tends to do today: the two ideas are separate, and the first is more prominent than the second. This disjunction in John's theory corresponds to the main peculiarity which confronts, and often puzzles, modern readers of Middle English 'literature'. There too, both in prose and in verse, we find that eloquence, the literary use of language, does not entail fictivity.

This is most obvious in the case of Middle English prose. Prose fiction, one of the three main branches of modern English literature, plays almost no part in Middle English. The Italian *novella* of the fourteenth century—Boccaccio's *Decameron*, for instance—represents a kind of short prose fiction which was imitated in France (the *nouvelle*), but hardly in England until after the end of the Middle Ages. We have already seen, too, that the fashion for long prose romances which arose in thirteenth-century France was not followed by English writers until the fifteenth century; and Malory's *Morte d'Arthur*, though commonly regarded as the first substantial work of prose fiction in English, does not fit easily into that familiar category. The criterion of fictivity is hard to apply here. Is Malory a chronicler or a writer of fiction? How far does he affirm the truth of the stories he tells? William Caxton, in the preface to his edition of the *Morte*, asserts the historicity of Arthur and couples Malory's work with the chronicles of the other Nine Worthies, but without claiming that the whole story is true *res gesta*: 'for to gyve fayth and byleve that al is trewe that is conteyned herin, ye be at your lyberté'.[14] In the event, readers have had no difficulty in accepting *Morte d'Arthur* as a fully literary text, since for most of them the question of 'fayth and byleve' scarcely arises, where Arthur's knights are concerned. So Malory, one might say, has at least *become* literature. Very few other Middle English prose works, however, can be assimilated so comfortably. To show this one has only to label some of the prose pieces which figure most prominently in the accepted canon of Middle English literature. *Ancrene Wisse* is a rule for anchoresses; *Sawles Warde* is a homily; *The Liflade ant te Passiun of Seinte Juliene* is a saint's life; *The Cloud of Unknowing* is a treatise on contemplation; Mandeville's *Travels* is (or purports to be) a travel book; *The Book of Margery Kempe* is a spiritual autobiography; *The Paston Letters* are letters.

Modern canons of literature, as I said before, have increasingly tended to exclude sermons, treatises, travel books, autobiographies, and other such specimens of non-fictional prose. In the case of Middle (and Old) English the strict application of this fictivity test would leave almost no prose literature at all. Yet many Middle English prose works which would be excluded on these grounds have a strong claim to be included on other grounds, because they plainly exhibit what Jakobson calls the 'poetic function' of language—a function which was not thought inconsistent, in those less specialized days, with practical intentions. Indeed, John of Garland speaks as if all kinds of true prose ought to be eloquent: the 'technigraphic' (used by writers such as Aristotle in exposition), the 'historial' (narrative, whether fictional or not), 'dictamen' (letters), and 'rithmus' (liturgical prose). It does not follow from this, of course, that all Middle English treatises, chronicles, and letters will exhibit the eloquence of which John speaks: 'pithy and elegant discourse, not in metre but divided by regular rhythms'. But a work such as *Ancrene Wisse* responds very readily to stylistic analysis. Such texts can safely be 'read as litera-ture'—provided only that one remembers not to take eloquence as a sign of fictivity.

The danger of forgetting that rule is much greater when one is reading Middle English verse. Unlike the prose, the verse of this period still forms a living part of our literature; and much of the best of it satisfies all modern criteria of *littérarité*. No one ever doubted the credentials of *Troilus* or *Sir Gawain and the Green Knight*. These poems lie somewhere near the centre of English, not just Middle English, literature. In them, the poetic use of language is associated with a richly fictive imagination. Not only do both poets treat their stories as *res fictae* (despite some unserious historical touches), but both exhibit a general displacement of discourse towards fictivity. They treat moral issues seriously, but in a distinctively literary way—not, in general, by direct didactic address to the reader, but by author and reader joining in absorbed contemplation of an imagined world. In *Sir Gawain*, final moral judgements are uttered, not by the author, but by Gawain, Bertilak, and the Round Table; and, since their judgements disagree, the ultimate effect is pleasingly oblique and non-affirmative. The only place in either poem where this displacement of moral discourse seems to break down is in the so-called epilogue to *Troilus*, which ends with moral advice addressed directly to the audience: 'Re-peyreth hom fro worldly vanyte . . .'. Although these lines express the most commonplace medieval sentiments, modern readers have found them hard to swallow, either dismissing them as an artistic blunder, or else taking them as expressing, in a displaced, fictive fashion, the struggle of a bewildered Narrator to make sense of his painful tale. Either reaction testifies to the power of Chaucer's fictive imagination in the rest of the poem. No other Middle English poet, indeed, comes as close as he does to our sense of the poet's peculiar vocation, both in what he does and what he does not do. It is significant that Chaucer and his friend and con-temporary John Gower are the first English writers known to have spoken of their Muse (*Troilus* II 6, *Envoy to Scogan* 38, *Confessio Amantis* VIII 3140).

But not all Middle English verse conforms so completely to modern notions of *littérarité*. The question may be simply one of quality: a piece of verse from any period may just be too crude and elementary to be con-sidered even bad literature. Much Middle English verse, however, raises a different question—one which, though not peculiar to medieval verse, has been prompted less and less often by verse in the modern period. In his Preface to the *Lyrical Ballads* Wordsworth wrote: 'It is supposed, that by the act of writing in verse an Author makes a formal engagement that he will gratify certain known habits of association, that he not only thus apprises the Reader that certain classes of ideas and expressions will be found in his book, but that others will be carefully excluded. This exponent or symbol held forth by metrical language must in different eras of literature have excited very different expectations'.[15] In modern times, and especially since Wordsworth's own day, the 'formal engagement' between the writer of verse and his public has come to exclude more and more firmly any expectation of direct, affirmative discourse, whether historical, moral, theological, philosophical, or scientific (the last scarcely imaginable). But the act of writing in verse did not in the Middle Ages set up such exclusive expectations. Verse was then still, one might say, a relatively familiar and workaday medium. True, the long process by which prose has progressively taken over the less literary functions of verse advanced several steps during the Middle Ages. One French writer says that he will not write the history of Troy 'in rhyme or in metre, for in them there is always of necessity much lying' ('par rimes ne par vers, o il covient par fine force avoir maintes mençognes');[16] but even this advanced view amounts to little more than the vulgar opinion that one cannot say what one means in verse because of the need to scan and rhyme. In England, more conservative in such matters than France, verse certainly did not carry a general 'exponent or symbol' of fictivity. We find sermons in verse, instructions for parish priests in verse, courtesy books and chronicles in verse, and even poems on alchemy stained with chemicals.

In his *Apology for Poetry*, Sidney distinguished the 'right poet' from the poet who deals with ethics, science, astronomy, and history. Of the latter kind of poet (he mentions, among others, Lucretius, the Virgil of the *Georgics*, Manilius, and Lucan) he remarks: 'because this second sort is wrapped within the fold of the proposed subject, and takes not the course of his own invention, whether they be properly poets or no let grammarians dispute'.[17] In *Troilus* or *Gawain* the poet clearly 'takes the course of his own invention', creating a poetic structure of marvellous integrity; but many Middle English poems belong to the second sort. The *Prick of Conscience*, which survives in more manuscript copies than any other Middle English poem, is simply a versified treatise on the wretchedness of life, the inevitability of death, and kindred subjects; and another huge Middle English 'poem', *Cursor Mundi*, traces the history of the world from Creation to Doomsday. Such works derive their structure from their 'proposed subjects'; and Ben Jonson would certainly have judged their authors 'not poets but versers, because they wrote not fiction'. We may be content, with Sidney, to leave grammarians to dispute whether the *Prick of Conscience* and the rest are literature or not. Future readers, taking a more distant, anthropological view of Western civilization, may be better placed to see the doctrine of the *Prick* and the history of the *Cursor* as themselves fictive or mythic creations (though not of their medieval authors) and so reabsorb them into the great spectacle of literature; but at present they are virtually excluded from the canon. There is no cause to quarrel with these exclusions. The difficulty arises with those works which lie somewhere between the two extremes represented by *Troilus* on one hand and *Cursor Mundi* on the other: poems such as *Pearl*, or *Piers Plowman*, or Dante's *Divine Comedy*. 'Right poems' these certainly are; yet they do not, or should not, settle as comfortably as do *Troilus* or *Gawain* into our category of literature. For one of the immediate objects of these poems is precisely *truth*—mainly theological truth, in the three cases mentioned—and they are capable of attacking that object with a directness which often makes the literary reader (that specialized modern creature) distinctly uneasy.

Consider *Pearl*, for instance. This is probably the work of the same anonymous poet who wrote *Sir Gawain*; and like that poem it exhibits in profusion the characteristics of *littérarité*. It belongs to a genre, the dream-vision, which more than any other allowed the medieval poet to 'take the course of his own invention', unconstrained by historical tradition. It exhibits an elaborate, autonomous structure, characteristic of works not 'wrapped within the fold of the proposed subject'. The poet's use of language is also highly, even extravagantly, poetic; and he exfoliates his main images and symbols, especially that of the pearl itself, in a fashion most congenial to modern criticism. Unlike *Gawain*, however, *Pearl* exhibits other characteristics which are likely to distract the strictly literary reader. I am not thinking here of the possibility (or rather probability) that the poem refers to a real event in the poet's life, the death of an infant daughter; for autobiography is the one form of non-fictive reference still generally allowed to the twentieth-century poet, and a modern reader who finds autobiographical reference in medieval poetry is more likely to be reassured than disturbed. The challenge comes rather from the poem's apparent claim to establish doctrinal truths—not comfortably broad truths about human nature and the like, but quite specific points of controverted Christian doctrine. The infant girl died before reaching the age of two, but after receiving the sacrament of baptism. She therefore died in a state of innocence, freed from original sin by baptism and not yet stained by sins of her own. Everyone in the poet's time agreed that the souls of such were saved; but the poem sets out to demonstrate a more controversial point: that such innocents are among the most blessed of blessed souls. This conclusion is established in the best medieval manner, by rational argument based upon authoritative texts: in this case, two biblical texts. The first is the parable of the vineyard, cited by the maiden to controvert the sceptical dreamer's objection that an infant, having had no opportunity to serve God on earth, could not possibly now be a queen in heaven. The other text is Chapter XIV of the Book of Revelation, describing St John's vision of the 144,000 *virgines* who follow the lamb in heaven. The maiden claims that, as an innocent, she has a place in that privileged company; and later the dreamer sees her in it.

It cannot be argued that the *Pearl*-poet, if he had *seriously* (to use Austin's word) intended to demonstrate his theological proposition, would have written a prose treatise. No one would want to suggest that *Pearl* is concerned only to establish its doctrinal point; but even the most literary of readers has to recognize, I think, that one of the immediate objects of the poem is theological truth. The poet is justifying the ways of God to man by applying reason to Scripture; and no medieval theologian could have proposed a surer way to truth than that. The poet certainly amplifies and adorns Christ's parable and John's vision; but the ornament is no more inconsistent with practical intention here than in medieval church furnishings, and the amplitude seems a witness to the poet's determination not to lose anything of the probative value of his texts.

It is the set towards doctrinal truth which presents the problem in poems like *Pearl*. We do not normally look for truth of that sort, our own or other people's, in poems. Dante's *Divine Comedy* presents the problem in a particularly acute form; and indeed it was the *Comedy* which provoked the first modern discussions of the matter, among humanist critics in sixteenth-century Italy. Dante, said Pietro Bembo, 'would have been a better poet than he in fact is if he had not attempted in his verses to appear as something other than a poet'.[18] Humanists such as Bembo found particular fault with Dante's numerous passages of naked philosophical and theological exposition; for how were such things to be reconciled with Aristotle's doctrine of poetic imitation? The problem is typical of the new age, and so is the answer which other more subtle Aristotelians gave. One of these, Giacopo Mazzoni, in a remarkable passage, attempted to extend the concept of imitation to include science, philosophy, and history: the true poet can deal with such matters, but the manner of his dealing will be distinctive.[19] Whereas the scientist, philosopher, and historian are concerned to 'teach and discover the truth of things', the poet, according to Mazzoni, seeks only to represent their ideas in an imitation, just as he might represent the actions of a warrior or the words of a messenger. Thus Dante, in so far as he is a true poet, offers the reader not arguments and ideas but *images* of arguments and ideas; and the reader, in so far as he is a true reader of poetry, will look not to be convinced by arguments but to be delighted by their imitation. Unlike Sidney, then, Mazzoni allows that 'right poets' may handle the arguments of philosophers and the rest, but only in the way of imitation, not affirmatively. In one form or another, this idea has been widely accepted in modern times. T. S. Eliot's *Four Quartets*, for instance, contains many passages of apparently pure philosophic statement; but readers do not, I think, take such passages quite straight, as they would if they were reading a treatise on time or incarnation. For this is a *poem*; and the 'exponent or symbol held forth by metrical language' today leads us to expect from poems not direct statements but rather what I. A. Richards called 'pseudo-statements'.

Such expectations are the result of a long and complex process by which in modern times the various functions of discourse (information, argument, amusement, and so on) have been increasingly separated out and assigned to different sorts of text. If we want history, we go to the History section of the library, not to the Literature or the Philosophy section. This division of labour among different sorts of text was considerably less far advanced in the Middle Ages. Hence, the specialized expectations of the modern reader will frequently distort his view of medieval literature. The most sophisticated criticism is often the most at fault here. Critics are often excessively eager, for instance, to insist that this or that passage of philosophical or theological exposition in a medieval poem is to be read 'dramatically'—as the expression, that is, of the partial point of view either of the Narrator (a favourite figure) or of some character in his story. Such imitation of ideas, of course, does occur, in medieval literature as elsewhere. The long speech in which Chaucer's Troilus argues the doctrine of predestination (IV 958-1078) should certainly be read dramatically, as a philosophical projection of the hero's distress at the prospect of losing Criseyde. It is, in fact, particularly characteristic of Chaucer to observe how people use the arguments which suit their immediate emotional or practical needs. More than any other Middle English poet, he treats ideas and arguments as objects of 'imitation' rather than affirmation; and that is one reason why he strikes us today as so very much the 'right poet'. Yet not even Chaucer can be completely contained within the limits of literature, however hard critics may try. The *Canterbury Tales* (in its surviving fragmentary form) ends with the *Parson's Tale* and Chaucer's *Retractation*. The *Parson's Tale* is a treatise on the sacrament of penance. The literary approach to the *Tale* will emphasize its appropriateness to its teller, a priest who would have administered the sacrament, and also its dramatic fitness as the last tale before the pilgrims enter the holy city of Canterbury; but such attempts to reabsorb the *Tale* into the *spectacle* of the Canterbury pilgrimage do not, I think, entirely convince the disinterested reader. Followed as it is by the *Retractation*, the *Parson's Tale* seems to break out of the fictional world of the poem and confront the reader directly with the realities of penance.

The trouble with realities, however, is that they tend to date. There is a passage in the *Divine Comedy* (*Paradiso* II) where Beatrice explains why there are spots on the moon. Those who insist, as I would, that to understand this passage fully one must realize that Dante thought he had the right answer to this problem and wanted to state it, will also have to confess that, in this case at least, he was hopelessly wrong. No doubt if he had seen what we have seen, he would have rewritten the passage. It is embarrassing to admit that a poem can suffer the indignity of such obsolescence; but better so than to pretend that medieval poets never affirm and therefore never get things wrong. The corpus of Middle English literature is substantial enough to satisfy most tastes; but it includes some works—*Pearl* or, most notably, *Piers Plowman*—which cannot be studied exclusively in terms of the modern notion of literature.

2 Writers, audiences, and readers

I

When the Angles, Saxons, and Jutes first came to this country in the fifth century after Christ, they already had an alphabet, the alphabet of runes. Knowledge of these, however, was confined to the rune-masters; and they used their skill only for special and limited purposes: magic spells, marks of ownership, commemorative inscriptions, and the like. There is no evidence that these pagan English writers ever attempted to inscribe the songs and stories recited by the storytellers and bards of their time. Alliterative poems there certainly were, and probably prose sagas too; but such literature had nothing to do with *litterae* or written characters. The life-cycle of an English vernacular poem in the pre-literate fifth or sixth centuries would therefore have been quite different from what we are used to today. It would have been conceived and composed orally—in the bard's head, that is, before and during the act of performance. That act of performance would also have constituted its only mode of publication. Indeed, the poem could only be said to exist at all so long as it, or a recognizable form of it, went on being sung or recited either by the original bard, or by members of his audience, or by their successors. When no one remembered it any longer, the poem died.

This must have been the life-cycle of many Anglo-Saxon poems; but one can only speculate about their character, for there is no way of recovering an oral poem once it is forgotten. The Anglo-Saxon poetry which does survive (little more than 30,000 lines in all) does so because it was written down, not by the rune-masters, but by their successors, the Christian scribes. The Roman conversion of the Anglo-Saxons is customarily dated from 597, the year in which Augustine established his mission at Canterbury; and as the various kingdoms of the English were Christianized, they received not only a new religion but also a new alphabet: the Latin alphabet of the Roman and Celtic church. The importance of this change lay not so much in the alphabet itself (hardly more convenient than the runic) as in the Christians' way of using it. For the Christians, writing had a wider range of functions than it ever acquired in pagan Germanic society. The Church had a sacred book; and the Latin Bible was already flanked by a considerable body of written commentary, treatises, sermons, and the like. The same scribes who wrote such texts, most often monks, also spent some of their time copying Latin poems, both Christian and classical; for the Church had inherited from late antiquity the assumption that poetry—poetry worthy of the name—was a *written* art. Homer may have been an oral poet; but Virgil most emphatically was not. Literature was already, in Augustan Rome, dependent upon literacy; and it continued to be so in the medieval Latin church.

It is not surprising, therefore, that the scriptoria of Anglo-Saxon monasteries and cathedrals eventually gave some attention also to the recording and copying of vernacular prose and verse. Vernacular sermons such as those composed by the monk Ælfric and prose treatises such as the translations associated with the name of King Alfred supplied suitable material. So did vernacular verse, provided that it was pious, or at least sufficiently sober and dignified. The four great codexes, or manuscript books, upon which modern knowledge of Anglo-Saxon poetry chiefly depends were all probably produced in the scriptoria of monasteries or cathedrals, round about the year 1000.[1] Even at that late date, however, some 400 years after Augustine's mission, the art of writing was evidently confined to quite a small segment of English society. The extent of literacy at this time is a matter of some controversy among historians; but it would appear that few people could read or write outside the monasteries and cathedrals. Even priests were often illiterate; and in lay society, despite King Alfred's ambitious scheme to educate the sons of wealthy freemen, literacy was not common. It must be assumed, therefore, that much Anglo-Saxon poetry right up to the time of the Norman Conquest was composed without benefit of letters. Such 'oral composition'—if parallels with modern non-literate societies can be trusted—would have been highly traditional in character, employing set patterns of expression ('formulae') adapted to the demands of the ancient alliterative metre.[2] Some scholars regard the extant Anglo-Saxon verse corpus as representing in all essentials this traditional art of the bard or *scop*; whereas others would attribute most of it to the monks themselves, ascribing the so-called 'oral features' to literary imitation of a non-literary style. Thus *Beowulf* may be considered either as a Homeric, oral epic or as a literary, Virgilian one. But whatever construction one puts on the facts, few would deny that some understanding of oral composition is necessary for the appreciation of Old English poetry.

These remarks about literacy and poetic composition before the Conquest will serve to introduce some further thoughts on the middleness of Middle English literature. It is well known that the introduction of printing in the later fifteenth century had profound consequences for the history of English literature, consequences which I shall consider in my last chapter; but for the moment we may dwell on some earlier changes in the production and distribution of books. These changes, which occurred chiefly in the twelfth and thirteenth centuries, serve to distinguish the Middle English period from what went before almost as sharply as the introduction of printing distinguishes it from what came after. They altered the circumstances of literary composition, and in particular they helped to alter the nature of English poetry.

There was no dramatic technical innovation in the twelfth century to compare with the coming of printing technology in the fifteenth. What happened was rather an enormous expansion, even an explosion, in the demand for books and written materials of all sorts.[3] From about 1100 onwards, the Church in Western Europe moved out of its monastic into its scholastic phase. The old cathedral schools expanded and were eventually joined by those new and dynamic institutions, the universities. New orders of monks, canons, and (from the early thirteenth century) friars, in the universities and elsewhere, pursued learning and research on a scale quite beyond the scholars of the Benedictine age. Secular clergy too, from archbishops down to rectors and vicars in parishes, became increasingly accustomed to the use of books and documents. At the same time, lay society was becoming more complex, and this increasing complexity required more and more paper-work of every sort. Bureaucrats and house-hold clerks, lawyers and merchants—such men became increasingly dependent upon written records and written instruments; and even those who had no immediate practical need to do so began to take more interest in books. King Alfred's prophetic vision of a governing class with direct access to the wisdom of the past through books took a step towards fulfilment among the Anglo-Norman families ruling England in the twelfth century.[4] Through their great households, where chaplains and clerks mingled with noblemen and their ladies, habits of literacy spread out into lay society, affecting, as time went on, the lesser nobility and the gentry.

New demands made by the Church, the universities, the professions and the gentry were met by a corresponding increase in the output of written material. This 'book revolution', as it has been called, was achieved in a variety of different ways: partly by a simple increase in manpower—more scribes, more illuminators, more binders, more parchment makers—and partly by improvements in productivity. Books came to be produced more rapidly and cheaply. Thus scribes developed, side by side with the old monastic book-hand, a new, quicker, less formal kind of writing (cursive script), which they used first in documents and then, from the thirteenth century, in books. They organized in university towns a system by which several scribes could copy at the same time from a single exemplar (the *pecia* system). By the fourteenth century, commercial book-producers were achieving in their shops something as near to the mass-production of books as was possible before printing. This mass-production was facilitated by a new material, paper, introduced from the Near East and increasingly preferred to parchment: the earliest surviving English documents and books written on paper date from about 1300. The results of such changes are hard to quantify exactly; but it could be argued that, although printing made a critical difference to the multiplication of texts, the fourteenth century already surpassed the tenth in this respect almost as much as it was itself to be surpassed by the sixteenth.

These changes help to account for some of the salient differences between Old and Middle English literature. Literary prose can hardly exist without writing; and, although some scholars find traces of an oral saga prose in one early entry in the *Anglo-Saxon Chronicle*, the greater part of surviving Anglo-Saxon prose was evidently composed, in the ninth and tenth centuries, by bishops, monks, and chaplains. Thus the known tradition of English prose is from the first in the hands of *writers*; and it develops more or less continuously from the Old into the Middle English period, displaying the influence of Latin throughout and absorbing French influence, when it came, without disruption. English poetry, on the other hand, began as an oral art; and the corpus of surviving Anglo-Saxon verse, whatever the exact origins of individual pieces, clearly displays many of the characteristics of unwritten composition: even a late piece like *The Battle of Maldon* (after 991) builds its alliterative line out of traditional phrases and alliterative collocations, like an oral poem. But by the end of the twelfth century, at latest, the possibility of oral composition can for all practical purposes be ignored. Writing about 1200, Laȝamon can still occasionally produce something quite like classical Old English alliterative verse:

> Laverd Drihten Crist, domes waldende,
> Midelarde mund, monnen frovre.

> (Caligula version, 12760–1)

> Lord Christ, ruler of judgement, protector of the world and help of men.

But the verse of the *Brut*, fine as the poem is in many ways, lacks the technical discipline of the *scop* or bard. When in his prologue Laȝamon describes how he wrote the poem, his account shows, for all its extraordinary archaic manner, just how remote this poet already is from 'oral composition'. He says that he took three books, laid them out before him, and turned their pages. Then:

> Fetheren he nom mid fingren, ond fiede on boc-felle,
> Ond tha sothere word sette to-gadere,
> Ond tha thre boc thrumde to are.   (Caligula, 26–8)

He took feathers in his fingers and applied them to book-skin and set down together the truer words and compressed those three books into one.

Not every line of Middle English verse, of course, was composed with quill or stylus in hand. Then as now poets could compose songs and ballads in their heads; and longer works, though nearly always written in the first instance, might undergo a degree of recomposition or decomposition in the heads of those who, as they recalled them, would cut, and change, and add lines and passages. But all the evidence suggests that Middle English literature is largely the work of men writing on parchment, wax tablets, or paper, and often, like Laȝamon, consulting the writings of others in the process. Laȝamon himself was a parish priest, his contemporary Brian of Lingen (probable author of *Ancrene Wisse*) was a canon,[5] Lydgate was a monk, Dunbar a chaplain, Langland a clerk in minor orders, Henryson a schoolmaster, Gower perhaps a lawyer, Hoccleve a clerk of the Privy Seal, Chaucer (among other things) a customs official. These are all occupations of a bookish sort. Just how bookish the life of such an author could be appears from a passage in Chaucer's *House of Fame*, where Jove's eagle is describing, rather contemptuously, the cloistered life which Chaucer led as controller of customs:

> 'For when thy labour doon al ys,
> And hast mad alle thy rekenynges,
> In stede of reste and newe thynges,
> Thou goost hom to thy hous anoon;
> And, also domb as any stoon,
> Thou sittest at another book
> Tyl fully daswed ys thy look.'   (652–8)

rekenynges] i.e. at the customs house   *daswed*] dazzled

Chaucer is an extreme case of bookishness—the phrase 'dumb as any stone' suggests that he did not even mutter to himself, as most medieval readers did—but most Middle English poets were far nearer to Chaucer than to any oral bard. The poetry of this period, like its prose, was produced by *writers*.

This conclusion will seem startling only to those whose notion of the Middle Ages is derived from romantic novels. However, the term 'writer' raises two further issues in this context. I have used it in the literal sense of 'one who inscribes letters upon a surface', the physical activity so palpably evoked in the passage quoted earlier from Laȝamon; but that is not, of course, the main signification of 'writer' today. For one thing, if a person nowadays says that he is a writer, he may be taken to mean that he makes a living by writing novels, biographies, travel books, and the like. No single Middle English author was in that sense a 'writer'. Of those mentioned in the last paragraph, only Hoccleve could be said to have made his living by the pen—and he, not as an author but as a clerk. Medieval society was capable in some areas of a surprising degree of specialization (the division of labour in book production, for instance, between the scribe who wrote the main text and the illuminator who did the big capitals); but there is no sign in England of the specialized, professional, vernacular 'writer'. Even Chaucer, in another sense perhaps the most professional of all Middle English authors, seems to have owed little, if any, of his livelihood to his writings. Historians find nothing to distinguish his official career from that of less gifted contemporaries; and he was buried in Westminster Abbey simply because that was where good servants of the king were buried.[6] There was no Poet's Corner in the fourteenth-century Abbey. Even Chaucer was a Sunday poet—Douanier Chaucer.

So when applying the term 'writer' to the Middle English period, one must try to avoid any suggestion of professionalism. There is also another way, subtler and more profound, in which the term may now be misleading. In modern times, texts may be produced in a number of different ways: by pen, or by typewriter, or by printing-press, or by various sorts of photocopier. The work of producing texts is shared out between these devices in a complex, shifting fashion; but one broad distinction can be made. Writing and typing are mostly used to produce new texts, or originals; and it is left to printing and photocopying to produce copies. Thus the physical act of writing now normally implies composition of some sort (though not necessarily of the creative sort associated with 'writers'). What is not composition is left to the compositor. This situation has been brought about gradually in modern times by typography and photography; and it differs radically from the situation in the Middle Ages, when writing had no technical alternative. Before printing, the physical act which produced originals was the same as that which produced copies. 'Writers' were responsible for both.

Scholars have recently drawn attention to a remarkable passage from St Bonaventure: from the fourth *quaestio* of his proem to his commentary on Peter Lombard's *Sentences*. The thirteenth-century Franciscan distinguishes four 'ways of making a book' (*modus faciendi librum*). The following translation does little justice to his crisp scholastic Latin:

There are four ways of making a book. Sometimes a man writes others' words, adding nothing and changing nothing; and he is simply called a scribe [*scriptor*]. Sometimes a man writes others' words, putting together passages which are not his own; and he is called a compiler [*compilator*]. Sometimes a man writes both others' words and his own, but with the others' words in prime place and his own added only for purposes of clarification; and he is called not an author but a commentator [*commentator*]. Sometimes a man writes both his own words and others', but with his own in prime place and others' added only for purposes of confirmation; and he should be called an author [*auctor*].[7]

Perhaps Bonaventure should have added the *translator*; but otherwise his scheme seems satisfyingly complete. One notices, however, that he does not place the *auctor*, as the logic of the scheme might suggest, at the opposite extreme from the *scriptor* or scribe; for even the *auctor* does not, as Bonaventure describes him, write only his own words. The scheme simply does not allow for that possibility: even *auctores* will write the words of others, if only 'added for purposes of confirmation'. Perhaps Bonaventure had in mind the Latin theologians, with their constant citation of earlier authorities; but his characterization of the *auctor*, taken in the context of his scheme, implies a general way of thinking eminently typical of the whole age before printing and radically unlike our own. Men 'make books' by writing. Some do no more than copy an existing text, or else combine existing texts into new compilations; others add words of their own, either 'for purposes of clarification' or else 'in prime place'. But all are *writers*. Scribes, compilers, commentators, and authors are all, in different ways, doing the same thing: making books.

Bonaventure's scheme combines into a single continuum two functions which seem fundamentally different to us: composition and the making of copies. Both were functions of the physical act of writing, and a writer could easily combine them. Indeed, the possible combinations were more various and complex than Bonaventure's formal scheme allows. The description of the *scriptor* as one who 'writes others' words, adding nothing and changing nothing', for instance, implies that the medieval scribe was like the modern compositor; but in practice he often behaves quite differently. He 'adds and changes' not only inadvertently, like the compositor, but also deliberately. He replaces obscure expressions with more familiar ones, omits and rewrites passages, and sometimes adds passages from other sources or even passages of his own composition. Thus a *scriptor* may also at times perform the functions of *compilator*, *commentator*, *translator*, and *auctor*. The textual tradition of Langland's *Piers Plowman* presents many cases of scribes too interested in their original to be content merely to transmit it. They 'add and change' quite deliberately, to fortify an idea or redirect a satiric thrust.

Editors speak in such cases of 'scribal interpolation'; but interpolations are often so far-reaching that one can no longer call them 'scribal', in the ordinary sense of that term. This happened in the case of Chaucer's *Canterbury Tales*. Chaucer left this work in a fragmentary state, far from finished: many of the pilgrims lacked tales, and some of the tales lacked 'links' (prologues or epilogues to connect them with their neighbours). This situation prompted those concerned with the transmission of the text to take drastic action. Someone found the *Tale of Gamelyn* for Chaucer's Cook (whose authentic tale breaks off after a few lines); someone else wrote a 'spurious link' to join the Tales of the Pardoner and the Shipman; and so on. Those concerned with the transmission of the text in modern times— the editors—exclude these passages or relegate them to the Textual Notes, because they are interested only in Chaucer; but it might be interesting also to have an edition of the *Canterbury Tales* which included the non-Chaucerian accretions in its text—not only *Gamelyn* and the spurious links, but also Lydgate's *Siege of Thebes*, a poem which attaches itself to the Canterbury pilgrimage by means of a pseudo-Chaucerian prologue. Such an eclectic edition would show us the *Tales* as they were most often read in the generations following Chaucer, and also provide much material for reflection on the function of *scriptores* in the age before printing.

The textual traditions of *Piers Plowman* and *Canterbury Tales* show how scribes, by 'adding and changing', take on functions which belong higher up on Bonaventure's scale. But there is also an opposite phenomenon. Just as the medieval *scriptor* was less specialized in his functions than the modern compositor, so the medieval *auctor* was less specialized than the modern author.

In the prologue to his *Brut*, Laȝamon says that, when he first conceived the idea of writing a history of the British, he travelled around and 'obtained those noble books which he took as his exemplars [*tha he to bisne nom*]'. These were, he says, the English book which St Bede made, a Latin book made by St Albin and Augustine, and a third book by a French clerk called Wace. He continues as follows:

> Laȝamon laid these books out and turned the pages. He looked at them lovingly—may God be merciful to him! He took feathers in his fingers and applied them to book-skin and set down together the truer words and compressed those three books into one.

I have already commented on the archaic character of this passage. Writing and reading are both described in starkly physical terms—turning pages, pressing a feather into skin. Laȝamon presents himself, in fact, as a penman making a book. His method is to 'compress' three existing books into a single new one. That description presents Laȝamon as a *compilator* rather than an *auctor*. Indeed, the use of the term *bisne* may imply an even humbler function. The *bisne* is a model or example for imitiation; and in this context it seems to suggest, not just a 'source', but the model which a copying scribe would follow—his exemplar.

Laȝamon's words illustrate vividly all those characteristics of medieval authorship which are most foreign to modern readers. Here we have an author who positively claims what his modern equivalent would be reluctant to admit—that he has made his book by copying from three others. How can he possibly *claim* such a thing? The passage itself suggests two answers. First, the poet's description of how he travelled widely throughout the land to find those 'noble books' which contained what he was looking for recalls the relative rarity of books in his day, and also the difficulty of tracking down and assembling what had been written on a particular subject, in this case the history of the British. So even if a writer ended up doing no more than produce a copy of an existing text, he could still claim to have done something useful; and if he succeeded in 'compressing three books into one', that was even more useful. Two centuries later, Thomas Hoccleve claims the same utility for his *Regement of Princes*—a treatise also, as it happens, drawn from three main sources:

> But unto you compile I this sentence,
> That, at the goode luste of your excellence,
> In short ye may behold and rede
> That in hem thre is skatered ferre in brede.   (2132–5)

this sentence] these ideas   *luste*] pleasure   *That . . . brede*] what is scattered far and wide in those three books

Laȝamon's other claim on the gratitude of his readers is implicit in his description of the three books which he compressed into one. Apart from the anticlimactic appearance of 'a French clerk called Wace' (omitted in the other manuscript of the *Brut*), the list would have appealed strongly to a contemporary reader's love of authorities, for it consists of three saints, all from the heroic early years of Christianity in England. What better exemplars could Laȝamon have found for his history of the British? Such an attitude to earlier authorities is highly characteristic of medieval writers in general. Authority belongs to the *auctor*—an honorific title, as even Bonaventure's cool account suggests. To be an *auctor* is to *augment* the knowledge and wisdom of humanity (both words derive from Latin *augere* 'increase'); and few latter-day writers can claim as much. The great *auctores* of the past, Christian and pagan, have already said almost everything there is to say. Chaucer expresses this common attitude in his

Prologue to the Legend of Good Women, using the image (traditional in this context) of gleaning:

> For wel I wot that folk han here-beforn
> Of makyng ropen, and lad awey the corn;
> And I come after, glenynge here and there,
> And am ful glad if I may fynde an ere
> Of any goodly word that they han left.   (G version, 61–5)

Of makyng ropen] reaped the harvest of poetry

In circumstances such as these, when the main harvest has already been reaped, it would seem that no writer need be ashamed to perform the lower functions on Bonaventure's scale. To make available the works of the great authors of the past, by compilation, translation, commentary, or even simple transcription was not an unworthy aim for a writer of that time. The 'noble books' of which Laȝamon speaks had more authority than a modern could ever claim for his own gleanings.

There is, however, one curious and cheering fact about Laȝamon's prologue which suggests that this analysis of the Middle English 'writer' is not yet complete. Laȝamon was not telling the truth. The 'English book which St Bede made' and the Latin one attributed to Albin and Augustine seem to be the Latin original and the Anglo-Saxon translation of Bede's *Ecclesiastical History*—a work to which the *Brut* owes only a single incident. The poem is, in fact, almost entirely based on Wace; but even here the relation between Laȝamon and his *bisne* is much less close than his own account would suggest. The English writer does much more than select and set down the 'truer words'. The very act of converting Wace's trim octosyllabic couplets into an alliterative verse still echoing with the heroic and melancholy music of the old bards is enough to ensure that the exploits of the British kings assume a gravity, and sometimes a ferocity, quite alien to the courtly Anglo-Norman manner. Laȝamon also makes many major additions, most remarkably to the long history of Arthur which forms the core of the book. Here we find, for instance, a series of powerful similes unparalleled—indeed inconceivable—in Wace. In the most famous of them, Arthur imagines his defeated enemy, Baldulf, looking down at his warriors lying dead in the river Avon:

> Nu he stant on hulle ond Avene bihaldeth,
> Hu ligeth i than stræme stelene fisces
> Mid sweorde bi-georede. Heore sund is awemmed;
> Heore scalen wleoteth swulc gold-fage sceldes,
> Ther fleoteth heore spiten swulc hit spæren weoren.
>
> (Caligula, 10639–43)

Now he stands on a hill and looks into the Avon, seeing how steel fishes lie in that stream, girt with sword. Their swimming is spoiled; their scales gleam like gold-plated shields, their fish-spines float there as if they were spears.

In these remarkable lines, the riddle of the steel fishes is resolved by a pair of similes which point backwards from the image (taken for reality) of the fishes to the reality (offered as an image) of the drowned warriors. If he had written nothing else, the passage would be enough to raise Laʒamon above the rank of mere translator or compiler.

The case of the *Brut* is quite typical. In this great age of the manuscript book, conditions encouraged a certain 'intertextuality' or interdependence of texts. Few works have the free-standing independence to which modern writers generally aspire; most are related to other texts by some degree of compilation, or translation, or even simple transcription. Yet in those works which still interest us this dependence upon other texts proves to be partially illusory. The writer himself will often encourage the illusion of dependence by assuming the role of translator or compiler when he is in fact writing his own words 'in prime place'. The creative act of the *auctor* is concealed from the reader, as if to protect or to excuse it. When Chaucer describes himself in his *Treatise on the Astrolabe* as nothing but a 'lewd compilator of the labour of olde astrologiens', his description may not be too wide of the mark; but the colophon at the end of the *Canterbury Tales* (perhaps not by Chaucer, admittedly) can be taken only as an indeterminate half- or quarter-truth: 'Heere is ended the book of the tales of Caunterbury, compiled by Geffrey Chaucer, of whos soule Jhesu Crist have mercy.'

Chaucer is particularly adept at exploiting, often for humorous effect, the possibilities of confusion between the various 'ways of making a book' distinguished by Bonaventure. In the proem to the second book of his *Troilus*, for instance, he calls on the muse of history, Cleo, to help him with his rhyming. No other help is necessary, he says, because he is doing no more than translate out of Latin:

> of no sentement I this endite,
> But out of Latyn in my tonge it write.

> Wherfore I nyl have neither thank ne blame
> Of al this werk, but prey yow mekely,
> Disblameth me, if any word be lame,
> For as myn auctour seyde, so sey I.   (II 13–18)

of no sentement] out of no personal experience   *endite*] compose

Chaucer has already referred to his Latin 'auctour' by the name of Lollius;

but this author has proved as elusive as Laȝamon's Albin and Augustine: he turns out, in fact, to be no more than a name deriving from a passage in Horace. Chaucer did have real sources—Boccaccio's *Filostrato*, mainly, and also two other versions of the Troy story by Benoit de St Maure and Guido delle Colonne—and in many places he does indeed translate from Boccaccio's Italian, sometimes conflating it with Benoit's French or Guido's Latin. With more justice than Laȝamon, he might have claimed to have 'compressed three books into one'. Yet his *Troilus* may claim to be one of the most original poems ever written in English. There had been nothing like it before in English; nor can it easily be matched in Latin, French, or Italian. Comparison with Boccaccio's poem reveals a new creation, within which even passages of direct translation are transfigured.

Chaucer's *Troilus* has a curious pendant in *The Legend of Good Women*, where the poet represents himself as accused by the God of Love of slandering women by telling the story of the faithless Criseyde. He is defended against this charge by Queen Alceste, who refers as follows to his 'translations' of the *Roman de la Rose* and the *Filostrato*:

> 'for that this man is nyce,
> He may translate a thyng in no malyce,
> But for he useth bokes for to make,
> And taketh non hed of what matere he take,
> Therfore he wrot the Rose and ek Crisseyde
> Of innocence, and nyste what he seyde.
> Or hym was boden make thilke tweye
> Of som persone, and durste it not withseye;
> For he hath write many a bok er this.
> He ne hath not don so grevously amys
> To translate that olde clerkes wryte.'   (G version, 340–50)

nyce] foolish   *useth*] is accustomed   *hed*] heed   *nyste*] did not know   *hym was boden*] he was commanded   *thilke*] those same   *withseye*] refuse

We do not believe in this foolish Chaucer. The 'innocent' note which he strikes here is all his own. We hear it again in the *Canterbury Tales*, before the *Miller's Tale* and after *Sir Thopas*. Yet, for all its ironies, the passage truly represents something of the circumstances under which even Chaucer worked. He speaks of himself as 'writing', not in the abstract, specialized sense of the modern word, but in the older general, physical sense. He employs his pen to make books: 'he useth bokes for to make' . . . 'he hath write many a bok er this'. Indeed, he claims (in comic self-defence) to have had no other purpose than the production of a book, as if he were a professional scribe. He takes orders; and he does not care—perhaps *taketh non hed* implies that he does not even notice—what he writes. In his guileless way, he will simply translate what 'olde clerkes' have written, with no intention other than to make a book.

II

It is commonly believed that almost all medieval literature is anonymous. Many of the writings are formally anonymous, in the simplest sense—the name of the author has been lost, and we are reduced to speaking of 'the author', or 'the *Gawain*-poet', or just 'Anon'—and even where the name of the author is known, we may think of his work as anonymous in a deeper sense. The authors of this period, we believe, rarely talk about themselves, and their works are most often unmarked by any distinctive personality. Their subjects are traditional, their styles conventional. Like medieval sculpture and architecture, in fact, medieval literature is supposed to be public, impersonal, monumental.

These large generalizations have as much truth as can reasonably be expected of them. Certainly much medieval writing *is* anonymous, both in the formal and the deeper sense; and it has been necessary for the modern reader to be thoroughly alerted to this anonymity—which he tends to find alien and disturbing, especially in poetry. However, well-intentioned scholarly warnings and explanations have proved so effective that many people now have a greatly exaggerated conception of the anonymity and impersonality of medieval literature, as if it were all, with trifling exceptions, quite faceless. Thus a helpful rough generalization has been taken for a universal truth. The truth, however, is more complex and interesting; and the right way to see that, at present, is to explore the ways in which medieval writings are *not* anonymous. This has been done for some medieval Latin writings by Peter Dronke in his book entitled *Poetic Individuality in the Middle Ages*. In the present section I shall consider Middle English writers from a similar point of view: To what extent, and under what conditions, do they display 'poetic individuality'?

Let us start with the apparently superficial question of formal anonymity. What requires explanation here is not the fact that some Middle English pieces are anonymous, but the fact that others are not. English literature attracted little comment in that age: there is virtually no biography or criticism, let alone journalism, to help with attributions. Nor did manuscript books begin with a title-page upon which the name of the author is prominently displayed, as became the custom with the coming of printing. Indeed the title-page, with its extravagant and formal layout, testifies to a sense of the identity of a text which would be hard to parallel in the English Middle Ages. 'What is it called?', we ask, and also (with a peculiar pregnant use of the preposition) 'Who is it *by*?' Many medieval books provide no answer to either question. The four poems commonly ascribed to the *Gawain*-poet, for instance, survive only in a manuscript in the British Library whose scribe simply wrote his texts out, without naming either them or their authors.

Manuscripts are not always so reticent, however. They do not have title-pages, but they may indicate title or author or both in a more unobtrusive fashion, either at the beginning of a text in an *incipit* ('here begins . .'), or at the end in an *explicit* ('here ends . .'). An example of an *explicit* longer and more circumstantial than that already quoted from the end of the *Canterbury Tales* occurs at the end of the edition of Malory's *Morte d'Arthur* printed by William Caxton (who was still observing the conventions of the manuscript age here):

> Here is the ende of the hoole book of kyng Arthur and of his noble knyghtes of the Rounde Table, that whan they were holé togyders there was ever an hondred and forty. And here is the ende of *The Deth of Arthur*. I praye you all jentylmen and jentylwymmen that redeth this book of Arthur and his knyghtes from the begynnyng to the endynge, praye for me whyle I am on lyve that God sende me good delyveraunce. And whan I am deed, I praye you all praye for my soule. For this book was ended the ninth yere of the reygne of Kyng Edward the Fourth, by Syr Thomas Maleoré, Knyght, as Jesu helpe hym for Hys grete myght, as he is the servaunt of Jesu bothe day and nyght.[8]

As in the Chaucer *explicit*, the first part provides a title, or rather something between a title and a description, for the 'book'. The rest announces the name and title of the author. It also implies something of his peculiar circumstances; for the request that readers pray for Malory's 'good delyveraunce' suggests what an *explicit* to an earlier part of the book plainly states: that the author was a 'knight prisoner' at the time of writing. There follows, as in the Chaucer *explicit*, a more conventional prayer for the author's soul.

These prayers are more significant than may at first appear. It is a curious fact that Middle English writers, when they announce their name and perhaps add some biographical particulars, do so most often in the context of some prayer or plea. These occur not only in *explicits* but also within the text itself; and here too authors are quite ready to name themselves. Paradoxically enough, authors' names actually occur more frequently in medieval texts—within the body of the text, that is—than in modern ones. In his treatise *The Convivio*, Dante remarks that 'rhetoricians forbid a man to speak of himself, except on needful occasions'; and Dante's own practice follows this rule. His name occurs only once in the text of the *Divine Comedy*, and then to great effect. At the very moment in the *Purgatorio* where the poet discovers that Virgil, his guide and master, is no longer by his side, Beatrice addresses him by name: 'Dante, weep no more for Virgil's going' (XXX 54-5).[9] Dante is now his own master, crowned and mitred over himself (XXVII 142); and the single use of his name signifies that new status as an independent person. But other medieval poets introduce their names more freely, on occasions which the modern reader would hardly consider 'needful'—most often in what may appear purely conventional prayers and pleas.

Yet these pleas and prayers provide the chief matrix within which what we would call 'autobiographical writing' first grows and develops in England. They take various forms. Medieval man considered himself to be dependent for his prosperity and happiness upon the grace and favour of those set above him; and one way to win such favour was to pray for it, either directly or through intercessors. The supreme source of favour was God. One could pray directly to God, or else pray others to intercede with him on one's behalf—other living men, or the saints in heaven, or the Virgin Mary. On earth the pattern was the same. Men who had favours to bestow, from kings and archbishops downwards, could be approached either directly or else indirectly through the good offices of some member of their household who himself enjoyed the lord's favour. Any such petition, whether to God or to some secular or ecclesiastical patron, would gain strength from a description of the petitioner's plight; but the really fundamental requirement was that the would-be beneficiary should be clearly and unambiguously identified—otherwise the favour might go to the wrong person.

This simple observation, which would seem to have little to do with poetic individuality of any sort, in fact goes a long way to explain why medieval writers name themselves when they do. It also helps to explain their characteristic manner of self-portraiture. They are discovered, as it were, upon their knees; and they speak of themselves most often, not in the pride of the poet, but in the humility of the petitioner. Their usual tone is one of complaint and of entreaty.

The only known poet from the Anglo-Saxon period to whom a substantial body of surviving verse can be attributed is Cynewulf. Cynewulf wove his name, spelled out in runic letters, into the closing passages of four poems. As Kenneth Sisam pointed out, his motive was the desire to be remembered by name in the prayers of others.[10] Thus at the end of *Juliana* he writes: 'I beg every man who repeats this poem to remember me *by name* in my need'. But Cynewulf gives little more than his name in these passages. His accompanying description of himself as a sinner, growing old and facing judgement, is highly conventional, in the manner of Anglo-

Saxon elegiac complaint. The monastic civilization of the ninth century was not favourable to poetic individuality. However, if we pass to the twelfth and thirteenth centuries, we find Early Middle English writers already beginning to fill out their petitionary passages with personal detail. The prologue to Laȝamon's *Brut*, from which I have already quoted, begins as follows: 'There was a priest among the people who was called Laȝamon. He was the son of Leovenath—may God be merciful to him! He lived at Arley, at a noble church, on the banks of the Severn'. The same prologue ends like this: 'Now Laȝamon prays each noble man, for the sake of almighty God, if he reads this book and learns these runes, that he utter faithful words for the soul of the father who brought him up and the soul of the mother who bore him and his own soul, that it may be the better for it'. Thus Laȝamon's account of how he wrote his book, though it may betray some pride in authorship, is framed by references to the author and his parents which are of a purely petitionary character.

The stiff formality of Laȝamon's third-person account of himself creates a distinctly archaic effect; but in another poem of about the same time we find a more flexible and personal development of the petitionary role. In *The Owl and the Nightingale*, quite early in the debate between the two birds, the Owl raises the question of who is going to act as judge between them. The Nightingale without hesitation proposes Master Nichol of Guildford—a man, she says, of great wisdom and discretion. The Owl accepts the proposal: when he was young, she says, Nicholas was somewhat wild and favoured nightingales; but now he is mature and steady in judgement ('ripe and fastrede') and therefore, she implies, will favour her. Much later in the poem, the Wren tells the two contestants where Nicholas is to be found, at Portesham in Dorset, and adds her own word in praise of his wisdom. It is a disgrace, she says, that bishops give livings to unworthy recipients and allow a man like Nicholas to live modestly in such a remote parish. The poem ends as the birds fly off to Portesham to receive Nicholas's judgement. According to the best recent opinion, Nicholas of Guildford was in fact the author of the poem. If so, *The Owl and the Nightingale* provides a subtle and amusingly shameless instance of petitionary autobiography. The object of this petition is not salvation but preferment, so the petitioner's merits can be described—and in a very human, even worldly, fashion. The ripeness of Nicholas places him, as it were, at the apex of an equilateral triangle, equidistant from the solemn Owl and the joyous Nightingale, and so acceptable to them both. The Owl's account suggests merely that Nicholas has followed a natural order of moral development in his life, from wild youth to settled maturity; but the fact that Nicholas proves equally acceptable to the Nightingale suggests that his present maturity is not of the kind that simply supersedes the joy of youth—rather, it includes that joy in a higher synthesis. Thus the two birds can join, with the Wren, to act as intercessors on behalf of Nicholas. The poet himself neither directly addresses the patron nor invites the reader to speak for him. His plea is conducted obliquely, within the fiction of the bird debate.

'The discovery of the individual was one of the most important cultural developments in the years between 1050 and 1200. It was not confined to any one group of thinkers. Its central features may be found in many different circles: a concern with self-discovery; an interest in the relations between people, and in the role of the individual within society; an assessment of people by their inner interests rather than by their external acts'.[11] These bold words of the historian Colin Morris sum up a view of the twelfth century which is shared by several recent writers on political, legal, and cultural history. In the Latin literature of that century, not least in England, one can find many signs of such a 'discovery of the individual'. E. R. Curtius points out that twelfth-century Latin writers frequently identify themselves by name and display an 'unadulterated pride of authorship', unlike their monastic predecessors.[12] It cannot be said, however, that Early Middle English literature provides any very striking instances of the 'discovery of the individual'. One would hardly cite Laȝamon as a case of 'unadulterated pride of authorship'; and the ideal of wise maturity which Nicholas of Guildford represents leaves little room for personal inflections or idiosyncrasies. The real discovery of the individual comes in English literature much later—with the great writers of the Ricardian period and their successors in the fifteenth century. The *Gawain*-poet preserves his anonymity; but his contemporaries, Chaucer, Langland, and Gower, are poets with names and identities who speak in distinctive voices. The same can be said of the next generation: Lydgate and Hoccleve, for instance. In this later medieval period, in fact, anonymity increasingly becomes characteristic of certain specific *types* of writing—ballad, for instance—while other types reveal more and more about their authors.

This increasingly personal character in Middle English writing from the mid-fourteenth century onwards has little or nothing to do with Renaissance humanism. Chaucer knew something of Petrarch and his works; but Italian humanism had little influence on him, and even less on his contemporaries; and even in the fifteenth century most English writings remain unlit by the dawn of the Renaissance. The origins of autobiographic and personal writing in this period lie nearer home, in the literary traditions of the Middle Ages. Surprisingly enough, in fact, the authors of this period continue to present themselves in the old petitionary attitudes. The image of the writer becomes fuller and more intimate, but its outlines are most often unchanged.

When Chaucer's fellow-Londoner Thomas Usk (d. 1388) registers his authorship of his Boethian prose treatise, *The Testament of Love*, he does so by making the opening letters of his chapters spell out this message: MARGARETE OF VIRTU HAVE MERCI ON THIN USK.[13] Here, as in Cynewulf's poems, the riddling form serves as a guarantee of the purity of the petitionary intent: it is as if only the receiver of the petition—in this case, perhaps, St Margaret—needs to know the author's name. A less pure example, more characteristic of its period, is provided by Chaucer's brilliant short poem, *Lenvoy de Chaucer a Scogan*. Chaucer here addresses a petition to his friend Scogan, a member of Richard II's household, asking him to put in a good word for him:

> Scogan, that knelest at the stremes hed
> Of grace, of alle honour and worthynesse,
> In th'ende of which strem I am dul as ded,
> Forgete in solytarie wildernesse,—
> Yet, Scogan, thenke on Tullius kyndenesse;
> Mynne thy frend, there it may fructyfye!
> Far-wel, and loke thow never eft Love dyffye.   (43–9)

Forgete] forgotten   *Tullius kyndenesse*] the friendship of which Cicero speaks   *Mynne . . . fructyfye*] recollect your friend in a place where recollection may bear fruit   *eft*] again

The urbane Horatian tone of this concluding stanza is typical of the poem. Chaucer speaks of himself as too old for love and even for poetry, living a dull and obscure life at Greenwich (according to a note in the manuscripts), while Scogan enjoys the favour of the great upstream at the court of Windsor. It seems churlish to insist upon the petitionary character of such a light and graceful piece; yet the beautiful image of Scogan kneeling at the head of a river which the poem converts from the prosaic Thames into the 'stream of grace' carries the unmistakable implication that he may act as intercessor for his friend. And just as the intimate and familiar style of the poem testifies to Chaucer's status as a friend, so the account of his life, 'dul as ded, forgete in solytarie wildernesse', testifies to his need for a friend's help. The petitionary intention gives to the autobiographical allusions their distinctive note. Nicholas of Guildford struck the same note in his account of his own obscure circumstances; and it remains characteristic of much later Middle English autobiographical writing—the note of complaint.

The most consistent exponent of this kind of writing was Chaucer's disciple, Thomas Hoccleve. Unlike John Lydgate, with whom his name is often linked, Hoccleve is an interesting and underrated writer; and much of the interest of his work derives from its rich autobiographical vein. The pattern of complaint and petition is exceptionally clear here. His autobiographical passages, much fuller and more detailed than Chaucer's, regularly form part of pleas for assistance, and they derive their character from this function. *La Male Regle de T. Hoccleve*,[14] for instance, may at first appear a purely personal confession; but Hoccleve's account of his ill-regulated life leads him to reflect not only on his broken health but also on his empty purse—'My body and purs been at ones seeke' (409)—and the poem ends with an appeal to Lord Fourneval, the Treasurer, to pay his overdue annuity. This is very far from the supposed anonymity of medieval poetry; but the vivid personal details are ordered towards a very medieval end: the petition to Fourneval. Thus Hoccleve describes how, after drinking in the City, he was reluctant to return on foot to the Privy Seal Office in Westminster, where he then lived and worked—in summer because of 'Heete and unlust [disinclination] and superfluitee', and in winter because the Strand was muddy:

> And in the wyntir, for the way was deep,
> Unto the brigge I dressid me also,
> And ther the bootmen took upon me keep,
> For they my riot kneewen fern ago.
> With hem was I itugged to and fro,
> So wel was him that I with wolde fare;
> For riot paieth largely everemo:
> He styntith nevere til his purs be bare.   (193–200)

dressid me] went   *took upon me keep*] took notice of me   *riot*] extravagance
fern] long   *So . . . fare*] it was so good for whoever I chose to go with

Thus a moral confession slides into a complaint for an empty purse.

Hoccleve, as a clerk in the Privy Seal Office, was further removed than his master Chaucer from the 'stremes hed of grace' at the king's court; but like Chaucer's, his work illustrates how dependence, even remote dependence, upon the favour of the king or his officers encouraged writers to display their individuality. Even what we would regard as the regular salary of an official such as Hoccleve might not be paid unless the Treasurer was reminded of his continuing existence. As Chaucer's Arcite cynically observes in the *Knight's Tale*:

> And therfore, at the kynges court, my brother,
> Ech man for hymself, ther is noon oother.   (I 1181–2)

In the earlier Middle English period the king and his ministers spoke French. Thus the writers who depended on the favour of Henry II, in the twelfth century, displayed their often very striking identities in French or Latin. In the latter part of the fourteenth century, however, English finally established itself at court; and it is surely significant that this development coincided with a real 'discovery of the individual' in English writings. Petitions to court play an important part in displaying the late medieval poet to his readers. Many examples are to be found in the works of the Scottish poet William Dunbar, who was attached to the court of James IV of Scotland (d. 1513). Like Hoccleve, Dunbar complains of his empty purse and petitions the Lord Treasurer; and even when he writes a free-standing personal poem, such as the delightful verses *On his Heid-Ake*, his tone of complaint suggests an unspoken petition. Dunbar's poetry illustrates even better than Chaucer's how the circumstances of court life fostered a sense of individuality—'Ech man for hymself, ther is noon oother'.

Poets could express this individuality in a variety of literary forms; but one especially favoured was the dream poem. In such poems the content of the dream is usually very artificial and literary, in the manner of the *Roman de la Rose*; but the conventions of the genre dictated that the dreamer, if identified at all, should be identified with the poet himself—by name, or biographical particulars, or both. We have already seen how Beatrice in the *Divine Comedy* addresses the dreamer, or rather visionary, just once as 'Dante'. No English poet can match the power of that moment; but the occasions when Ricardian poets identify themselves in dreamer or narrator are none the less highly characteristic and interesting.

Very often we recognize the familiar pattern of complaint and petition, but adapted here to the fictional world of the dream. I have already referred to the scene in Chaucer's *Prologue to the Legend of Good Women* where Queen Alceste presents to the angry God of Love a petition on behalf of Chaucer, naming not the poet himself but his works:

> he wrot the Rose and ek Crisseyde
> Of innocence, and nyste what he seyde. . .

This fictive scene does not, as in *The Owl and the Nightingale*, mask a real petition: at most, Chaucer is asking the ladies to forgive him for his portrait of Criseyde. Yet here once more we discover the poet on his knees, dependent upon the will of a great lord and the good offices of a friend at court. As in *Scogan*, Chaucer treats his own art with self-depreciating irony, playing the traditional role of poet-petitioner with a style all his own.

Gower's *Confessio Amantis* provides a parallel to Chaucer's *Legend*. *Confessio Amantis* is not a dream poem, because its narrator does not fall asleep; but it belongs to the dream-poem tradition in many ways, not least in its manner of identifying narrator with author. Towards the end of the poem, the narrator Amans has completed his confession and writes a letter of petition to Venus and Cupid, asking to be relieved of his sufferings in love. His confessor, the priest Genius, presents the petition on his behalf, and Venus pays him a visit:

> To grounde I fell upon mi kne,
> And preide hire forto do me grace:
> Sche caste hire chiere upon mi face,
> And as it were halvinge a game
> Sche axeth me what is mi name.
> 'Ma dame,' I seide, 'John Gower.'
> 'Now John,' quod sche . . .   (VIII 2316–22)

chiere] gaze   *halvinge a game*] half in jest

Up to this point in the poem, Amans has been portrayed, with great skill and delicacy, as a very conventional courtly lover; but here he is identified by name with the poet. And it is precisely at the moment of his petition to Venus that 'Amans' becomes 'John Gower'. In the speech which follows, Venus makes the first reference to the fact that the narrator is old and ill ('suche olde sieke', 2368). This sad fact colours the beautiful ending which follows, in which the narrator is cured of his love-malady and returns soberly home at a soft pace. Gower was himself old at the time of writing (VIII 3130); and he here allows the image of his true situation to show through the delicate courtly fiction of Amans, Venus, and the rest. The petition itself belongs entirely to the fiction; but here as in Chaucer's *Scogan* it serves to establish the distinctive minor key in which both these poets speak of themselves—a key of complaint, apology, and ironical self-depreciation.

Chaucer and Gower belong to the first generation of English writers who form a group of recognizable people. Another member of this group is William Langland. Langland's *Piers Plowman* is a dream poem of a different sort from Chaucer's. Although it owes something to the *Roman de la Rose*, its main affiliations are with a different tradition of French dream poetry: a kind of non-courtly, religious allegory, best represented by a once widely-read early fourteenth-century writer by the name of Guillaume de Deguileville, author of *Pèlerinage de la Vie Humaine*. Court petition has no part in such work; and when Langland, like his contemporaries, writes himself into his poem, it is to different effect.

Langland's dreamer is called Will. Many passages in the poem suggest that this is to be taken as an abstract allegorical name, like 'Conscience': Will represents the moral will, and also the human quality of wilfulness. But he is also clearly William Langland. The poet indicates his full name when he has Will say, in mildly cryptic fashion: 'I have lyved in londe . . . my name is Longe Wille' (B XV 152). Thus Will Langland introduces himself into his poem both as a moral agent (will) and as an object of moral censure (wilfulness); and it is in passages of confessional self-examination that his full presence is felt. One of these passages represents the high water mark in the 'discovery of the individual' by medieval English writers.[15]

One of the many original features about *Piers Plowman* is that it consists of a series of dreams separated by waking intervals. In one of these intervals, between the first and second dreams, Langland's final revision (the C Text) introduced a scene in which Will meets Reason and Conscience.[16] The episode begins with Will waking from the dream of Lady Meed, in which Conscience and Reason first appeared to him:

> Thus y awakede, woet god, whan y wonede in Cornehull,
> Kytte and y in a cote, yclothed as a lollare,
> And lytel ylet by, leveth me for sothe,
> Amonges lollares of Londone and lewede ermytes,
> For y made of tho men as resoun me tauhte.   (C V 1–5)

woet god] God knows   *wonede*] lived   *cote*] cottage   *lollare*] idler   *lytel ylet by*] thought little of   *lewede*] ignorant   *made of*] wrote about

When Chaucer gives particulars of this sort, as he does in the *House of Fame*, it is sometimes possible to confirm them by biographical evidence; but no such evidence is available in the present case. However, sceptical criticism has produced no good reasons to doubt that Langland is portraying his own circumstances at the time of writing. It is perhaps no more than mildly interesting to learn of Langland living in modest circumstances with his wife in Cornhill, a few hundred yards from Chaucer; but what follows strikes a deeper personal note. When Will says that he 'composed verses [*made*] about those men as reason dictated', he both identifies himself as the author and claims the traditional right of the moralist to speak the truth regardless of what the world may say. But his encounter with Reason and Conscience, which follows immediately, presents Will in a very different light. Conscience and Reason are not, like Chaucer's Cupid or Gower's Venus, great ones to whom the poet addresses his petitions and complaints. Their relation to Will is rather that of confessor to penitent—almost, in modern terms, interrogator to victim—and the effect of their questioning is to subject the moralist's own way of life to searching moral scrutiny. Langland was a clerk in minor orders. He made a living for himself, on the evidence of this passage, by saying prayers for the souls of living patrons and of the dead, both in London and elsewhere. It is this irregular and dubious way of life that the moralist attempts, in a passage of marvellous richness, to defend against his questioners. In that 'hot harvest' (when the working year was at its height) Will struggles to prove to Reason that his own work is more legitimate than that of the beggars and idlers which it so uncomfortably resembles. His arguments are strained and unconvincing. He is too weak and tall to work in the fields, he says; and anyway he is a *clerk*, and clerks have their own kind of work, different from that of mere labourers and more pleasing to Christ:

> 'Preyeres of a parfit man and penaunce discret
> Is the levest labour that oure lord pleseth.'   (84–5)

levest] most acceptable

Conscience punctures this rhetoric with a dry comment: 'By Crist, y can nat se this lyeth'. Conscience 'cannot see that this is relevant' because, as he says, a life of unregulated begging is not 'parfitnesse'. At this point, Will seems to crack, confessing that he *has* wasted his life; yet even this beautiful and moving speech ends in a declaration of good intentions which the poet recognizes as still suspect:

> 'So hope y to have of hym that is almyghty
> A gobet of his grace, and bigynne a tyme
> That alle tymes of my tyme to profit shal turne.'
> 'Y rede the,' quod Resoun tho, 'rape the to bigynne
> The lyif that is louable and leele to thy soule'—
> 'Ye, and contynue,' quod Conscience . . .   (99–104)

gobet] scrap   *rede*] advise   *tho*] then   *rape the*] make haste   *louable*] praiseworthy   *leele to*] lawful for

Such autobiographical passages in Ricardian poets and their successors often, unlike Laȝamon's prologue, stand in an intimate relation to the works which contain them. The reader of *Piers Plowman*, coming upon the passage in Passus V in the C text, recognizes that it does indeed reveal the author of the poem he is reading; for he already knows the same Langland—digressively indignant, sometimes aggressively self-righteous, but also capable of a noble honesty which does not spare his own favourite ideas and solutions. The corresponding passages in Chaucer and Gower are much less frank—but then that too is characteristic. When Chaucer speaks of himself, he displays the same personality which is implicit in the rest of his poetry—in the 'innocent' tone, especially, which gives to the irony its peculiar, personal flavour. These medieval writers, at least, are in no sense anonymous.

III

So far in this chapter I have been concerned with writers: how they presented themselves in their works, and what it meant in that period to be a 'writer'. Let us now turn to the audiences who listened to the writings and the readers who read them. The fundamental difference here between medieval and modern conditions can be simply stated. People in the Middle Ages treated books rather as musical scores are treated today. The normal thing to do with a written literary text, that is, was to *perform* it, by reading or chanting it aloud. Reading was a kind of performance. Even the solitary reader most often read aloud, or at least muttered, the words of his text—performing it to himself, as it were—and most reading was not solitary. The performance of a text was most often a social occasion. These occasions took many forms, depending upon the social setting and the nature of the text. In all classes of society what we would now call 'lyrics' were commonly sung and also, in the case of the 'carol', danced to. Sermons and devotional writings were preached from the pulpit and read aloud in the houses of the devout. Minstrels (Chaucer calls them 'gestours') told tales and sang songs at peasant festivities and also in the houses of the great. In the latter, too, members of the household read aloud to small parties of friends. Chaucer describes such an occasion in his *Troilus*, in a scene where Pandarus visits Criseyde:

> he forth in gan pace,
> And fond two othere ladys sete, and she,
> Withinne a paved parlour, and they thre
> Herden a mayden reden hem the geste
> Of the siege of Thebes, while hem leste.
>
> Quod Pandarus, 'Madame, God yow see,
> With al youre fayre book and compaignie!'   (II 80–86)

geste] story *hem leste*] it pleased them *yow see*] watch over you

That coupling of 'book' and 'company' speaks of a world which is lost; but the modern reader, in his silence and solitude, can at least imagine the differences and reflect upon them.

Undoubtedly the best way to realize almost any medieval text, prose or especially verse, is to read it aloud or hear it read. The second-best way is to read as far as possible in the manner of a silent score-reader, allowing the sounds to speak to the inner ear. All poetry speaks to the inner ear; but medieval poetry—and also much of the prose—was addressed to that more robust instrument, the outer ear. The writers composed most often for the performing voice—speaking, intoning, chanting or singing—and the ex-

pressive effects which they contrived tended in consequence to be boldly
and emphatically shaped for the voice to convey to the ear. Here is a fine
example, from Chaucer's portrait of the Summoner in his *General Prologue*:

> And if he foond owher a good felawe,
> He wolde techen him to have noon awe
> In swich caas of the ercedekenes curs,
> But if a mannes soule were in his purs;
> For in his purs he sholde ypunysshed be.
> 'Purs is the ercedekenes helle,' seyde he.
>
> (*Canterbury Tales* I 653–8)

ercedekenes] archdeacon's

The conventions of the printed page require editors to open inverted
commas somewhere in the last three lines; but, as often with Middle
English writings, the lighter and less explicit pointing of the scribes, who
do not use inverted commas, corresponds better to the realities of performance, in which the voice passes gradually from the indirect speech of the
opening to the direct speech of the close. The voice will also bring out the
full effect of the word 'purse', as it moves from rhyme position, through
medial position, to an emphatic place at the beginning of the last line,
where its explosive effect is strengthened by the fact that all the five
preceding lines have begun with weakly stressed grammatical words. The
explosion expresses the Summoner's contempt for the gullible faithful,
and also a kind of angry admiration for the archdeacon and his racket.

Few readers, however deeply silent, could fail to catch at least something of the boldly vocal effect of this passage. Our chief inadequacy as
readers, in fact, lies not so much in response to such dramatic writing for
the voice, as in response to the more formal and patterned effects which
medieval writers devised for their performers: effects of rhyme,
assonance, alliteration, parallelism, and the like. Plain uneloquent speech
consists, in principle, of a string of words governed only by demands of
sense and by the rules of grammar and syntax. The art of eloquence
consists partly in stamping patterns of similar forms and sounds upon such
amorphous sequences, so that the ear can perceive order in what would
otherwise be just one thing after another. Such formal patterns, which do
not necessarily have any specific dramatic or expressive function, are on
the whole more boldly prominent in medieval than in modern literature.
They are a source of regularity and order in prose as well as in verse.
Indeed, the distinction between verse and prose—never as clear to the ear
as it is to the eye—tends to be neutralized by the art of eloquence, which
seeks to establish similar patterns in both:

O helle, deathes hus, wununge of wanunge, of grure ant of granunge, heatel ham ant heard wan of ealle wontreathes, buri of bale ant bold of eavereuch bitternesse, thu lathest lont of alle, thu dorc stude ifullet of alle dreorinesses.[17]

O hell, death's house, dwelling of wailing, of shock and of shrieking, cruel home and harsh abode of all distress, city of sorrow and residence of wretchedness, you most hateful of all lands, you dark place full of all miseries.

This passage from the Early Middle English homily *Sawles Warde* would certainly have won the admiration of rhetoricians such as John of Garland. When the words are read aloud, as they should be, the alliterations and assonances may seem overdone; but the modern reader will perhaps tolerate them as expressions of the horror of hell. Our chief difficulty comes with patterns which lack that expressive justification. These we tend simply not to hear, as a listener could not fail to hear them. Such purely formal patterns may be regarded as belonging to the rhetoric of the spoken word: they aid the reciter's memory and the listener's comprehension. Silent readers tend to suppress or ignore them; and this is particularly damaging to older writings. The most obvious example of such a formal pattern is rhyme in verse. When Chaucer speaks of 'rymyng craftily' (*Canterbury Tales* II 48), he refers to an aspect of his art which evidently engaged his serious attention. No treatises on vernacular poetry survive from medieval England; but fourteenth- and fifteenth-century French writings known as 'arts of second rhetoric' codify a poetic technique not unlike Chaucer's;[18] and in these books the craft of rhyming plays a prominent part. Chaucer shared with his French contemporaries a connoisseur's ear for rhyme. The elaborately-wrought opening paragraph of the *Canterbury Tales*, for instance, is finished off with a kind of rhyme which was then thought the most excellent of all—punning rhyme:

> The hooly blisful martir for to seke,
> That hem hath holpen whan that they were seeke. (I 17–18)

It is a mark of incompetence in such matters that our ear generally fails to hear a distinction between such 'rime equivocque' and mere flat repetition of the same word—a base trick, the latter, which Chaucer parodies in *Sir Thopas*.

Regarding rhyme as a purely formal matter, we tend to ignore it and so miss, not only the various pleasure of likeness-in-difference, but also such expressive effects as the rhymes may sometimes have. With alliterative verse, the case is just the opposite. In post-medieval English poetry, alliteration is an expressive option, not a formal requirement; so whenever alliteration is used, we look for expressive effects, often of a muscular sort ('rebuffed the big wind'). But in poems such as *Sir Gawain* or *Piers Plowman*, alliteration is a *formal* requirement, like end-rhyme in Chaucer. The alliterative line is held together by internal head-rhyme: 'Amonges *l*ollares of *L*ondone and *l*ewede ermytes'. So readers nowadays, who expect too little of Chaucer's rhymes, tend to expect too much of the alliterations of alliterative poets. These poets do, of course, quite often use alliteration expressively, as in this pair of lines from the alliterative *Wars of Alexander*, describing a thick oriental mist:

> Thai ware umbethonrid in that thede with slike a thike cloude
> That thai might fele it with thaire fiste, as flabband webbis.[19]

> They were wrapped about in that country with such a thick mist
> that they could feel it with their hand, like flapping cobwebs.

But the norm in all these poems, including *Sir Gawain*, is for alliteration to function as a purely formal patterning of the speech-sounds; and that is how the inner ear should learn to take it, unless there is positive reason to the contrary.

Thus Middle English literature requires the silent reader to resist, if he can, the tyranny of the eye and to *hear*. Certain of the writings, we may now add, make a further requirement. They treat the reader, not just as a hearer, but as a member of an audience or group of hearers. This is not, as might be supposed, an inevitable feature of any text produced for oral delivery. Old English poetry, whether or not it was orally composed, was certainly intended for oral performance; yet *Beowulf*, after acknowledging the audience in its opening line ('Lo, we have heard . . .'), pays them almost no attention thereafter. This is typical of surviving Old English verse, and also prose. Middle English writers are very much more inclined, in general, to address themselves explicitly to their hearers; and in some kinds of writing—sermons in prose, tales and romances in verse, especially—the set towards the audience can become very marked. Even the *Gawain*-poet, the most formal and impersonal of the great Ricardian poets, occasionally allows himself a freedom of address to the audience which would be unthinkable in *Beowulf*, as at the end of the Third Fitt, where he takes his leave of the hero, lying in bed on the eve of his encounter at the Green Chapel, with the following words:

> Let hym lye there stille,
> He has nere that he soght;
> And ye wyl a whyle be stylle
> I schal telle yow how thay wroght.   (1994–7)

> *He . . . soght*] he has nearly got what he was looking for   *And*] if

Such addresses to the audience naturally take different forms according to the kind of audience addressed. Some lyrical and devotional works, for instance, are addressed to a single person. Thus the author of the fourteenth-century mystical treatise, *The Cloud of Unknowing*, directs it to a young 'spiritual friend' who himself aspires to the mystical experience. This is not merely a token dedication. The manner of the whole work accords with the ideal of spiritual friendship, as it was derived from Cicero's *De Amicitia* in the twelfth century by writers such as St Bernard. The tone is solicitous without being overbearing, warm without indulgence; and the loose, informal structure of the book matches the familiar, epistolary style. Chaucer commands a secular version of the same intimate manner, in his epistolary poem to Scogan (where he refers to Cicero's treatise); but his poems more often address themselves to a group than to an individual. In *Troilus* especially there are many passages which imply the presence of a polite audience, listening with expert ear to the poet's tale of courtly loving. The poet even anticipates their criticism at one point. He has just described how Criseyde first looked with favour at Troilus:

> Now myghte som envious jangle thus:
> 'This was a sodeyn love; how myght it be
> That she so lightly loved Troilus,
> Right for the firste syghte, ye, parde?'
> Now whoso seith so, mote he nevere ythe! . . .
>
> For I sey nought that she so sodeynly
> Yaf hym hire love, but that she gan enclyne
> To like hym first, and I have told yow whi.

(II 666–70, 673–5)

parde] by God   *mote he nevere ythe*] may he never prosper

Here the imaginary interruption prompts Chaucer to a reply which reveals how close he already was to engaging in conversation with his audience. A frontispiece to an early manuscript of *Troilus* shows Chaucer in a kind of pulpit apparently reading to a large audience of ladies and gentlemen;[20] but the manner of the poem itself suggests a less formal and public sort of performance—like the private reading in Criseyde's own paved parlour, perhaps.

Most Middle English romances, however, were written for an audience considerably less select and discriminating than Chaucer's, and the manner of their performance was no doubt different too. Metrical romances such as *Havelok*, *Beves of Hampton*, or *Libeaus Desconus*, whatever the

exact status of their authors, could easily have formed part of the repertoire
of a minstrel entertainer or 'gestour'. They are rather baldly rhymed,
either in short couplets or in tail-rhyme stanzas; and they employ many
oaths, asseverations, and clichés—all simply designed, unlike the oral
formulae of Old English, to dilute the narrative and make for easy listening. This is a poetry of everyday entertainment which has no equivalent
today. The opening of *Havelok* illustrates the manner:

> Herkneth to me, gode men,
> Wives, maydnes, and alle men,
> Of a tale ich you wil telle,
> Hwo-so it wile here, and ther-to dwelle.
> The tale of Havelok is i-maked;
> Hwil he was litel, he yede ful naked.
> Havelok was a ful god gome,
> He was ful god in everi trome,
> He was the wihtest man at nede
> That thurte riden on ani stede.
> That ye mowen now y-here,
> And the tale ye mowen y-lere.
> At the beginning of ure tale,
> Fil me a cuppe of ful god ale.   (1–14)

ther-to dwelle] wait to hear it   *yede*] went   *gome*] man   *trome*] armed
force   *wihtest*] most stalwart   *thurte*] might   *y-lere*] learn

Oral communication tends to require more redundant elements than does
written communication: where it may be sufficient to write a thing once,
we often say it twice—especially at the beginning of an exchange, where
the listener may not yet have tuned in to our way of talking. These opening
lines from *Havelok* show how written texts intended for oral performance
may exhibit the same high degree of redundancy. 'Alle men' in the second
line does nothing except achieve a flat identical rhyme and make nonsense
of 'gode' in the first. The couplet in lines 7–8 asserts the same thing twice,
with virtually no increment of meaning in the second line; and the same
criticism can be made of lines 11–12.

The opening flourishes of *Havelok* represent the manner of Middle
English writing at its slackest. Fortunately not all the literature of the
period—indeed, not all *Havelok*—is like this. However, even the best of
it—even Chaucer—often strikes the reader of Donne, Pope, or T. S. Eliot
as relatively loose and uneconomical. Middle English poets are at their best
in long, narrative pieces, composed in an easy long-distance style. What
we remember of their work is not often the highly condensed image or
pithy phrase. One of the few *lines* most people remember from Chaucer is

'Allone, withouten any compaignye'; but the eloquence of even that line is hard to appreciate outside its contexts (*Canterbury Tales* I 2779 and 3204). In itself, indeed, it is hardly less redundant than the worst lines in a minstrel romance.

It seems, then, that almost all Middle English writings betray the influence of 'oral delivery', if not in passages of direct address to the audience, then at any rate in the general constitution of their style. But the English writings of this period were not written exclusively for the ear. As was pointed out earlier, the years between 1100 and 1500 saw a great increase in literacy; and this meant, not only that more people could read and write, but also that they became more and more dependent on those skills. One important stage in the latter process is reached when the solitary reader finally relinquishes his dependence upon sound. The old way of reading, known in the monasteries as *rumination*, was a slow and noisy process—an audible 'chewing over' of the precious words of the text. Only when the text is finally silenced does reading cease to be a performance. Chaucer, as already noted, testifies to having reached that advanced degree of literacy:

> also domb as any stoon,
> Thou sittest at another book.   (*House of Fame* 656–7)

Chaucer moved in circles where such dumbness must have been unusually common. I refer not so much to the court society of Westminster or Eltham as to the circles of educated men in the city of London: officials like Chaucer himself and Hoccleve, lawyers from the Inns of Court, and clerks from Oxford and Cambridge. Such men would represent the high water mark of literacy in their day; and they are certainly to be thought of as readers much in the modern way, with books at their bed's head like Chaucer's Clerk of Oxenford, not as members of a listening audience. At the end of *Troilus*, Chaucer submits the poem to the judgements of two such men—the scholarly poet John Gower, and Ralph Strode, a Fellow of Merton College who was also a London lawyer:

> O moral Gower, this book I directe
> To the and to the, philosophical Strode,
> To vouchen sauf, ther nede is, to correcte,
> Of youre benignites and zeles goode.   (V 1856–9)

This passage evokes a picture of Gower and Strode as individual readers ('to *the* and to *the*') poring over the text of *Troilus*—a picture unlike that of a listening audience evoked by the passage quoted earlier ('Now myghte som envious jangle thus . . .'). But both pictures, I believe, represent part of the truth; and the contradiction between them accurately indicates the situation in which Chaucer, Gower, and their immediate successors found themselves. The vernacular poetic tradition which these writers inherited was adapted in a multitude of ways to the practice of oral delivery; and that practice was still widespread in their day, not only in popular circles but also in polite society. But men like Chaucer, Gower, or Hoccleve were not minstrel entertainers: they were more like what in modern times would be called men of letters. However often their works might be read aloud, their own habits of reading were surely solitary and silent. These writers therefore found themselves partially alienated from their native literary heritage, in so far as that heritage represented conditions that were recessive in their day.

It would be a complex and difficult matter to trace the responses of late Middle English poets to this alienation. There seem to be two main kinds of response. First, there is the long and laborious process by which, as readers took over from audiences, the poets, consciously or otherwise, set about purging their work of redundancies adapted to the listening ear. Imitation of foreign literatures played an important part in this process; for French and Latin poetry offered many models for a literary way of writing far removed from the minstrelisms of *Havelok*. The *Confessio Amantis* of Gower, who himself wrote in French and Latin as well as English, shows how an English style modelled on French could achieve an undoubted polish and correctness, being purged (though at the cost of a certain debility) of minstrel features. This is the 'critical cultivation of his native language' for which Gower was justly praised by the eighteenth-century critic Thomas Warton.

Chaucer's response differed from Gower's in that he was more inclined to adapt and accommodate minstrel features than to purge them. His shrewdness and inventiveness in this matter appear best in the *Canterbury Tales*. His mocking apology for the *Miller's Tale* seems to address both a reader and an audience:

> And therfore, whoso list it nat yheere,
> Turne over the leef and chese another tale. (I 3176–7)

'Yheere' suggests a listening audience; but the next line affords a glimpse of the private reader, at leisure to select whatever in the book he fancies. In the *Canterbury Tales*, Chaucer resolves this discrepancy between audience and reader by taking the audience into the poem and leaving the reader outside. The fact that the tales are told by pilgrims to an audience of fellow-pilgrims on the road to Canterbury serves, as it were, to internalize and fictionalize the older face-to-face relation between narrator and audience, so that all those stylistic features which imply that relation gain a new lease of life. Addresses to the audience, oaths, asseverations, redundant phrases—such things become positively effective again in the new context, once they are directed, not by the poet at his reader, but by the fictional narrator at his equally fictional audience. In this way Chaucer was able to come to terms with much in the English poetic tradition which Gower rejected. Unlike Gower, he can speak 'ful brode' when he wants to.

However, it is Chaucer, not Gower, who provides the most striking proof of just how remote these new poets considered their work to be from that of their more naïve predecessors. Chaucer's *Sir Thopas* is a wicked parody of an old-fashioned minstrel performance. The opening may be compared with the opening of *Havelok*, quoted earlier:

> Listeth, lordes, in good entent,
> And I wol telle verrayment
> Of myrthe and of solas;
> Al of a knyght was fair and gent
> In bataille and in tourneyment,
> His name was sire Thopas.   (*Canterbury Tales* VII 712–7)

> *in good entent*] with attention   *verrayment*] truly   *gent*] gracious

The flattering address to the listening audience ('lordes'), the rhyming asseveration ('verrayment'), the weak doublet ('myrthe and solas'), the verbal rubble ('Al'), the stereotyped and inappropriate epithets ('fair and gent') could all be paralleled many times over in the tail-rhyme romances. These things represent, at its very worst, the age of orally recited poetry which was already, in Chaucer's day, beginning to recede into the past.

3 Major genres

Many people feel uneasy with the notion of genre. The word may conjure up visions of scholars pedantically sorting and labelling the works of dead writers, or, worse still, prescribing for living ones the rules of Tragedy or the Short Story. But there is a more profitable way of looking at the matter. We may see genre as one manifestation—the prime manifestation in literature—of a principle which governs all human communication, and indeed all perception. At its most fundamental, the principle simply states that perception involves identification. The very act of seeing or hearing, insofar as it is not purely physiological, is itself an act of interpretation. We decide what sort of thing we are seeing or hearing; and that identification in turn governs what we see or hear. Many visual tricks and puzzles illustrate this principle of perception: the line-drawing, for instance, which can be seen either as a rabbit or as a duck.[1]

Linguistic communication employs this principle at several different levels. At the level of whole utterances—which is where the question of genre chiefly arises—speakers and writers construct utterances which can be recognized and construed by readers and listeners as utterances of a certain *kind*. Each of these kinds has characteristics which native speakers readily learn to respond to as signals of a certain sort of meaning—the sort of meaning appropriate to a command, a road sign, a sonnet, a summons, or a joke, or a riddle. 'A: What is the difference between an elephant and a letterbox? B: I don't know. A: I won't send *you* to post a letter.' The pathos of this exchange derives from the fact that B is fully justified in construing A's question as a riddle. The question is pointless in any ordinary context; and its phrasing follows the conventions of riddle (which prescribe that one should say 'Why is a P like a Q?' but 'What is the difference between an X and a Y?'). Both form and content show clearly what kind of utterance this ought to be; and it is therefore very unfair of A to pretend that he was in fact asking a practical sort of question.

The riddle is a very formal type of utterance—more so than the joke, for instance, and much more than the anecdote. On the whole, literary types, or genres, tend to have this same set and formal character. Their function, however, is essentially the same as that of any other discourse-type: they establish for the reader, more or less precisely, what kinds of meaning he may expect to find in a text. It follows from this functional definition that genres are best regarded as historical phenomena—sets of conventions which shift and re-form from time to time, not abstract categories into which any text from any period should fit. Every age, perhaps, has its own system of genres, a hierarchy in which some kinds are dominant (the epic in the seventeenth century, the novel in the nineteenth) and others recessive (narrative verse in the twentieth). In what follows, I shall attempt a partial sketch of the 'system of genres' which characterizes Middle English literature, concentrating on major genres and on 'literature'; but it will be necessary to bear in mind the general continuity and overlap between literary genres and other discourse-types, and also the particular difficulty, discussed in the first chapter, of sorting Middle English texts into literary and non-literary.

I

In the course of the 1370s, Chaucer travelled twice to Italy; and it was evidently on these journeys that he became the first English writer to make the acquaintance of Italian poetry. He was deeply impressed by what he found in the poetry of Dante, Boccaccio, and Petrarch; but he also found much which he either could not or would not imitate. His reactions both positive and negative reveal a great deal about Chaucer himself, and also about the literary culture of England in his day. In particular, his reaction to Boccaccio's grand and ambitious poem *Il Teseida* displays a fundamental fact about the system of genres prevailing in Middle English.

Boccaccio's *Teseida*, written about the year 1340, deserves to be better recognized as a landmark in the history of Western literature; for it represents the first full-scale attempt by a vernacular writer to imitate Classical epic, and so stands at the beginning of a long line of Renaissance and post-Renaissance neo-classical heroic poems.[2] Boccaccio's title declares his ambition: this is to be an epic of Theseus, just as Virgil's *Aeneid* was an epic of Aeneas, or Statius' *Thebaid* an epic of Thebes. Like those two great Latin models, Boccaccio's poem is divided into twelve books. It even has (in some manuscripts, at least) exactly the same number of lines as the *Aeneid*: 9896. The main story—familiar to readers of Chaucer as the Knight's tale of Palamon and Arcite—is a conventional romance of young love, not much like anything in Statius or Virgil; but Boccaccio takes every opportunity to imitate the epic feats of arms so frequent in those authors— in Theseus' campaign against the Amazons, for instance, or in the great tournament at the end of the story. He claims, indeed, to be the first Italian poet to treat the labours of Mars in 'bello stilo'. 'Bello stilo' here means high, epic style: invocations, long epic similes, catalogues of warriors, oratorical speeches, and the rest. Boccaccio even went to the length of supplying his own notes, in imitation of those which accompanied medieval texts of Statius and Virgil.

Chaucer was more impressed with *Il Teseida* than most modern readers have been. Perhaps he saw in it confirmation of his own sense that vernacular poetry might after all be capable of matching the art and dignity of the classical *auctores*. In his *Troilus* he cultivated at times a high style which owed much—in its invocations, for instance, and in its periphrastic indications of time—to the epic *bello stilo* of Boccaccio. Yet, despite an invocation to Calliope, the Muse of Epic (III 45), *Troilus* cannot be called an epic; and when Chaucer came to make his own version of the story of Palamon and Arcite in the *Canterbury Tales*, he produced something even less like the classical type. Perhaps he considered that the story did not lend itself to epic treatment; and in any case he could hardly have allowed a Canterbury Tale to run to 10,000 lines. Yet the significant fact remains: Chaucer never followed Boccaccio in his attempt to re-create a prime classical genre in a modern vernacular. The enterprise was new and exciting—it was to be a favourite in Renaissance times—but its novelty seems not to have excited Chaucer.

The *Knight's Tale* is in many ways a unique poem; but in its generic relation to the *Teseida* it can be taken as representative. Middle English writers almost never follow the genre-system of Classical literature. Some of them, like Chaucer, had read a good deal of Classical Latin—Virgil, Ovid, Statius, Lucan, Seneca, and others. From such *auctores* they readily took ideas, stories, devices, phrases, and images. Unlike medieval Latin writers, however, English writers did not at this time attempt epic, satirical epistle, pastoral, ode, or any other of the major Classical forms. Their favoured genres are of native, or at least of medieval, growth. About these they were not much inclined to theorize, and some of them seem very ill-defined. Vernacular genre-terminology was certainly very defective. Yet, if one can forget about the familiar but inappropriate Classical categories, it is possible to make out the outlines of a very different system.

Drama provides an example. The fundamental modern generic distinction here, that between comedy and tragedy, goes back to ancient Greece and owes much to Aristotle's *Poetics*. As we have seen, the *Poetics* was little known in the Middle Ages, and direct knowledge of Classical drama was largely confined to the comedies of Terence, which were school texts, together with some comedies of Plautus and an occasional tragedy by Seneca. Greek drama was not read. It is not surprising, then, that the two Classical terms 'tragedy' and 'comedy' shifted their meaning in the Middle Ages. Chaucer, like Dante, used them to distinguish two types of non-dramatic narrative, one beginning happily and ending in misery, the other beginning in misery and ending happily: he calls *Troilus* 'litel myn tragedye' (V 1786). Neither term is ever used in Middle English to refer to contemporary drama; and that drama in fact exhibits a generic structure quite different from that suggested by the comedy/tragedy antithesis.

The fundamental generic distinction in what survives of Middle English drama lies between the mystery play and the morality play. The mystery plays (sometimes known as 'miracle plays') are chiefly represented by four cycles which survive, in varying degrees of disrepair, from Chester, York, Wakefield, and 'N town'.[3] Of the moralities, only five survive from before about 1500, of which the best known are *The Castle of Perseverance* and *Everyman* (the latter translated from the Dutch).[4] These plays baffle any attempt to decide whether they are comedies or tragedies. In the medieval sense of the term they are all comedies, for they all end happily. The mystery cycles trace the history of man's salvation from the Creation and the Fall through various Old Testament episodes (Noah's ark, Abraham and Isaac, etc.) to the life of Christ and the Last Judgement—a happy ending in which the vicious are damned and the virtuous saved. The morality plays trace a similar trajectory in the experience of the individual: the representative hero ('Everyman' or 'Humanum Genus' or 'Mankind') recovers by repentance and grace from his own personal Fall, and at the end of the play his soul is saved. Yet one would hardly nowadays call any of these plays comedies. It is true that both types of play have some farcical action and verbal humour in them, sometimes of a very broad kind, chiefly associated with evil characters such as Cain, the crucifying soldiers, the Sins and devils; but this comedy occurs in a context of serious, even tragic events—the killing of Abel, the Crucifixion, the corruption of Humanum Genus. All the plays, in fact, seem ready to pass at any moment across the great frontier between Comedy and Tragedy as if it were not there—which indeed it was not.

All familiar tragedy/comedy oppositions are neutralized in medieval English drama. Oppositions between serious and comic events, high and low characters, happy and unhappy endings lack the generic significance we commonly ascribe to them. Instead, the main generic distinction is based on an opposition between two kinds of *time*: historical time, in which the Fall and Redemption of mankind takes place; and the lifetime of the individual, in which he too falls and may be redeemed. The most comprehensive of the surviving morality plays, *The Castle of Perseverance*, follows its hero, Humanum Genus, from birth through a twice-repeated sequence of sin and repentance to a virtuous death. This is the equivalent, in morality time, of the full mystery cycle, which treats history in an equally comprehensive fashion, from Creation to Judgement. Other moralities concentrate on single episodes from the same typical life-history: the early *Pride of Life* and the late *Everyman* both deal with the approach of Death. Although the two types of play both address themselves to the same basic themes—sin, repentance, and salvation—they are clearly distinct from a literary point of view. There is, for instance, almost no overlap between their *dramatis personae*. Mystery plays are peopled for the most part with named individuals from scriptural history: Adam, Noah, Abraham, Christ, or Herod. Morality plays, by contrast, deal in personifications: the Seven Deadly Sins, Wisdom, Mercy, or Death. One set of characters lives in historical time, the other in everyday time; and the few characters who appear in both types of play change accordingly. Thus, in mystery plays, the Devil plays his various appointed historical roles, as rebel angel, tempter of Eve and Christ, victim of Christ's Harrowing of Hell, and receiver of the damned souls at Judgement Day; but in *The Castle of Perseverance*, the Devil takes his place in the everyday world of Humanum Genus as one member of that timeless triad, the World, the Flesh, and the Devil. Thus a character ostensibly the same will be different in different genres. A prince is not the same thing in one of Shakespeare's History Plays as in a fairy tale.

I have used the terms 'mystery' and 'morality'; but neither term would have been used by the original audiences or the authors, for both were adapted from the French by eighteenth-century antiquaries. *Everyman* calls itself a 'moral play'; but the only genre word applied to plays at all often by medieval English writers is 'miracle', and that popular word appears to have had no precise meaning at all. This apparent paucity and imprecision in the original terminology for dramatic genres (themselves quite clearly defined) is typical of medieval vernacular literature as a whole. We shall find the same difficulty with the lyric, and even with those major genres of narrative verse which occupy the dominant place in the Middle English genre-system. The notions of genre which govern the writings of this period are rarely articulated in the surviving texts, and then only in imprecise and often ambiguous terms. This is one sign of a general absence of articulate critical thinking about vernacular literature. No critical document of any sort survives from this period in English—nothing corresponding to Dante's *De Vulgari Eloquentia* in Italy, or the French treatises on poetry known as 'arts of second rhetoric'. English literature would appear to have had no critical tradition of its own until the sixteenth century. Poems such as *Sir Gawain*, *Troilus*, or *Confessio Amantis* could hardly have been produced by men who had not thought profoundly about the art of English poesy; but Gower, Chaucer, the *Gawain*-poet, and others like them must have felt that their native art, by comparison with that of regular Latin writers especially, was unregulated and disorderly.

Lack of order is nowhere more apparent than in the large and varied body of work commonly known as the Middle English Lyric.[5] The term 'lyric' in this context usually means no more than a short poem, preferably in stanzas—as in R. T. Davies's anthology entitled *Medieval English Lyrics*—but it is hardly possible to speak in general about 'lyrics' so loosely defined. In the present discussion I shall confine myself to short poems which speak in the first person, usually to a second person:

> Your yen two wol slee me sodenly;
> I may the beautee of hem not sustene,
> So woundeth hit thourghout my herte kene.

That wonderfully singing start to one of Chaucer's roundels illustrates the most characteristic *axis* of lyric poetry: the 'I' addressing the 'you'. That mode of address is rarely dominant in other kinds of poem. The narrator who addresses the audience in Middle English narrative makes only sporadic appearances. 'First-person narrative' (where, as in *Great Expectations*, the story is told in the first person by one of the characters) plays little part in medieval literature, except in the case of dream poetry—and dream poems betray a kinship with lyric, both by their adoption of lyric motifs and by their easy incorporation of actual lyrics.

First-person poetry is not the same thing as personal poetry. The Oxford Dictionary says that lyric poetry 'directly expresses the poet's own thoughts and sentiments'; but that description is quite inapplicable to the lyric poetry of the English Middle Ages. Indeed, one might argue that the poet's own thoughts and sentiments found direct expression *less* often in lyrics than in other kinds of writing. None of Chaucer's works is more inscrutably impersonal than the roundel just quoted, with its polished conventional imagery of the lover's heart wounded by a shaft from his lady's eyes. To say 'I' in a poem of this kind is not, as in ordinary conversation, normally to refer to oneself. The first- and second-person pronouns are governed by the rules of a special poetic grammar: their significance varies according to the type of lyric in which they occur. A brief account of some of these variations will show how recognizing the genre is inseparable from understanding the significance.

In many medieval first-person poems, the 'I' speaks not for an individual but for a type. The speaker is to be understood not as the poet himself, nor as any other individual speaker, but as a lover, a penitent sinner, or a devotee of the Virgin. Such lyrics offered themselves to be used by any amorous, or penitent, or devout reader for his own individual devotions, or confession, or wooing; and there is a good deal of evidence that they were indeed appropriated by individual readers in just this way. The reading or singing of a religious lyric could constitute a real individual act of meditation, contrition, or devotion, just as the love poems of Chaucer could be used by lovers to express their own sentiments. A single speaking look during the performance of a love song might be enough to identify the mistress with the 'you' of the poem.

Chaucer's roundel is a good example of such a love poem. Let me now quote it entire:

> Your yen two wol slee me sodenly;
> I may the beautee of hem not sustene,
> So woundeth hit thourghout my herte kene.
>
> And but your word wol helen hastily
> My hertes wounde, while that hit is grene,
> Your yen two wol slee me sodenly;
> I may the beautee of hem not sustene.
>
> Upon my trouthe I sey you feithfully
> That ye ben of my lyf and deeth the quene;
> For with my deeth the trouthe shal be sene.
> Your yen two wol slee me sodenly;
> I may the beautee of hem not sustene,
> So woundeth hit thourghout my herte kene.

The roundel or *rondeau* was one of the so-called 'fixed forms' of lyric which were developed in the earlier fourteenth century by French poets, especially the poet-musician Guillaume de Machaut.[6] Chaucer was the first English poet to practise these fixed forms (which also included the ballade and the virelay), thus establishing a tradition which lasted in England until the time of Sir Thomas Wyatt. The forms were not confined to any particular subject-matter; but Chaucer himself evidently associated them chiefly with love. When Queen Alceste, in the *Prologue to the Legend of Good Women*, defends Chaucer against the charge of being 'mortal foe' to Cupid, she claims that he has in fact added to the glory of the God of Love with his writings, including:

> many an ympne for your halydayes,
> That highten balades, roundeles, vyrelayes.   (G version, 410–11)

ympne] hymn   *highten*] are called

The conventional terminology of the mock religion of Love ('hymns' and 'holy days') here points to a real analogy between secular and religious lyrics. Just as a Christian could speak to God through a hymn on a holy day, a lover could speak to his mistress at a feast or holiday through a love song such as Chaucer's 'Your Eyen Two'. Guillaume de Machaut, in his

Voir-Dit or 'True Tale', represents himself as using love poetry in this fashion; and John Stevens, in his excellent study of the social functions of courtly love lyric *Music and Poetry in the Early Tudor Court*, cites an English instance from Chaucer's *Franklin's Tale*. The young squire Aurelius has fallen in love with Dorigen:

> He was despeyred; no thyng dorste he seye,
> Save in his songes somwhat wolde he wreye
> His wo, as in a general compleynyng;
> He seyde he lovede, and was biloved no thyng.
> Of swich matere made he manye layes,
> Songes, compleintes, roundels, virelayes.

(Canterbury Tales V 943–8)

wreye] conceal

In the twelfth and thirteenth centuries English had produced nothing to match the high courtly love lyric, then in its heyday in Provence and France; but in their imitations of the fixed forms of a later period, writers like Chaucer were at last able, in their own now polite vernacular, to rival their continental contemporaries. The result is first-person poetry of a highly conventional sort, in which the lover addresses his mistress in the language of a 'general compleynyng'. Chaucer's roundel, for instance, is woven out of two traditional courtly images: the mistress is the queen, to whom the lover owes faithful service (7–9); and she is the enemy, who can kill the lover with a look (1–3). These two sets of images do not, as one might expect in a poem by Donne, interact to produce wit and paradox; the poem in fact concentrates not on the queen-enemy but on the servant-victim, and so avoids complications. The lover speaks in tones of simple supplication and surrender, as befits the speaker in this genre of lyric complaint.

In religious lyrics, we often find a similar kind of first-person speaker. In her book *The English Religious Lyric in the Middle Ages*, Rosemary Woolf argues that these are most often 'meditative poems', drawing the following distinction between them and the religious lyrics of the seventeenth century: 'The writers of both draw upon the contemporary methods of meditation of their respective periods, meditation on the Passion and, to a lesser extent, meditation on death. But, whereas the seventeenth-century poets show the poet meditating, the medieval writers provide versified meditations which others may use: in one the meditator is the poet; in the other the meditator is the reader' (p. 6). Here is an early example of such a first-person, 'usable' meditation on the Passion (No. 6 in Davies's anthology):

Now goth sonne under wod:
Me reweth, Marye, thy faire rode.
Now goth sonne under tre:
Me reweth, Marye, thy sone and thee.

Me reweth . . . rode] I feel pity, Mary, for your fair countenance

These lines (probably a complete poem) are recorded by an early thir-teenth-century Anglo-Norman writer in the course of a meditation on the Passion. He imagines Mary, at the moment when Christ commits her to the care of St John, speaking words from the Song of Songs (1:6): 'Look not upon me, because I am black, because the sun hath looked upon me'. The English lines, which follow, invite the reader to imagine the scene at sunset on the same day, and to appropriate the poet's expression of pity ('me reweth') to his own use. The poem is powerful because of its bold combination of physical with metaphysical: Mary's 'black' complexion ('rode') at the end of a long day in the fierce sun, sunburn felt most painfully at sunset, the sun setting behind the 'wood' or 'tree' (both terms emphasizing the physical reality of the cross); but also Christ as the Sun (*sol justitiae*, sun of justice) setting in death, and perhaps, too, Christ after his death descending into Hell.

'Now Goth Sonne' and 'Your Eyen Two' illustrate types of secular and religious lyric—the courtly love complaint and the meditation on the Passion—which employ what might be called the 'generic I'. They are both, in their different ways, 'general compleynyngs'. Other kinds of Middle English lyric are more specific: they require the reader not to identify with but to *identify* the first-person speaker. Dramatic lyrics of this sort are common in the period. A number of secular poems, for instance, speak in the voice of a young woman who complains that she has been rejected or betrayed by her lover. These belong to a common European type, known as the *chanson de femme*. Often they portray quite specific dramatic situations. One Middle English *chanson de femme* (No. 73 in Davies's anthology) begins like this:

Kyrie, so kyrie,
Jankin singeth merye,
With Aleison.

As I went on Yol Day
In oure prosession,
Knew I joly Jankin
By his mery ton,
Kyrieleyson.

Jankin began the offis
On the Yol Day,
And yit me thinketh it dos me good
So merye gan he say,
'Kyrieleyson'.

Kyrie . . . Aleison] Kyrie eleison, Lord have mercy on us (from the Mass, with pun on Alison) *Yol*] Christmas *ton*] singing *offis*] Introit of the Mass

It is remarkable, when one comes to think of it, how swiftly and decisively such a poem establishes in its opening lines what kind of person is speaking and what kind of thing, in this sort of poem, she is likely to say. In this particular version of the familiar theme of love-in-a-church, the speaker is evidently a woman. Her use of the familiar first person plural in '*oure* prosession' (a variant of the colloquial idiom known as the 'domestic *our*') acts as a generic marker, suggesting the world of the village or small provincial town. The following line reinforces this suggestion, for 'jolly' is not an epithet used in this way in high courtly contexts, and 'Jankin' is a familiar diminutive name most often bestowed on village gallants. The social setting and the linguistic register are exactly matched in Chaucer's *Wife of Bath's Prologue*. The Wife's fifth husband was also called Jankin; and she refers to him as 'Jankyn, *oure* clerk' (III 595) and as 'this *joly* clerk, Jankyn' (III 628). Both Jankins, as it turns out, are parish clerks.

This little dramatic lyric raises questions about the relationship between literary genre and social class in this period. In her relatively humble status, Jankin's admirer is typical of most speakers in *chansons de femme*, both English and French; and this fact has led some critics to treat these *chansons* as themselves products and expressions of a lower social world. Perhaps some of them were indeed popular products; but that conclusion cannot be reached merely by observing that their speakers are not great ladies. *Chansons de femme* deal in the complaints of women rejected or betrayed by their lovers ('Alas! I go with childe' are the last words of Jankin's sweetheart); and one has only to imagine the *grandes dames* of courtly love lyric uttering such complaints to see that it would not do. Considerations of decorum, in short, are quite enough to explain the modest social settings of *chansons de femme*; and those settings therefore prove nothing about the social *origins* of the poems, whether courtly or popular or both. From a literary point of view, in any case, it is the internal, generic relation between literary forms and social class which counts for most, not the external, sociological relation. We shall never know whether 'As I Went on Yol Day' was composed by a Jankin, or for Jankins; but at least we can see why it was written about a Jankin. The selection of that name was governed by the conventional internal logic of genre. A similar logic, as will be seen in the next section, determined the social setting of Chaucer's *Miller's Tale*: that fabliau contrasts with a romance such as the *Knight's Tale* much as a *chanson de femme* contrasts with a courtly love lyric, not because it was written for or by different kinds of people, but because it is a different kind of poem.

The *chanson de femme* is just one of several kinds of dramatic first-person lyric in Middle English, each with its own identifying features and its own internal logic. Another clearly defined secular type is the *chanson d'aventure*, in which the speaker rides out and encounters another person, who herself (it is usually a woman) may sing a *chanson de femme*. Thus poem No. 19 in Davies's anthology begins like this:

> Now springes the spray,
> All for love I am so seek
> That slepen I ne may.

> Als I me rode this endre day
> O' my pleyinge,
> Seih I whar a litel may
> Began to singe,
> 'The clot him clinge!
> Way es him i' love-longinge
> Shall libben ay!'

> *Now . . . spray*] now that the branches are coming into leaf *seek*] sick *this endre day*] the other day *may*] maid *The clot him clinge*] may the earth (of the grave) cling to him *Way*] woe *libben*] live

The *chanson d'aventure* is a genre which commonly identifies itself by means of a characteristic first line. A lyric which begins (after the refrain or burden) with the words 'Als I me rode this endre day' can hardly fail to be a *chanson d'aventure*.

Many religious lyrics of the first-person, dramatic variety declare themselves equally decisively. Poems in which Christ himself speaks from the cross, for instance, mostly fall into clearly defined types based, as religious poetry of this period so often is, upon passages from the Bible, the liturgy of the Church, or Latin devotional writers. One such type derives from a verse in the Lamentations of Jeremiah (1:12): 'Is it nothing to you, all ye that pass by? behold, and see if there be any sorrow like unto my sorrow'. As listeners to Handel's *Messiah* will know, Jeremiah's words were understood prophetically and put in the mouth of the crucified Christ. They were in fact used in the liturgy for Good Friday. Here (complete) is a Middle English complaint of Christ belonging to this type (Davies No. 46):

Ye that pasen by the weiye,
Abidet a little stounde.
Beholdet, all my felawes,
Yef any me lik is founde.
To the tre with nailes thre
Wol fast I hange bounde;
With a spere all thoru my side
To mine herte is mad a wounde.

stounde] time   *Wol*] very

Such a poem might be used in several different ways—in a sermon, or in a Passion play, or in conjunction with a picture of Christ on the cross, either in a manuscript or on a church wall—but even in complete isolation it would have been instantly recognized for what it was.

It would be unfortunate, however, if these selected examples left the impression that every single Middle English lyric belonged to some clearly defined and thoroughly understood type. Among the first-person lyrics, we find some in which the speaker is neither the all-purpose lover or religious devotee of the generic type, nor an identifiable *dramatis persona* as in the *chanson de femme* or the complaint of Christ:

> Ich am of Irlaunde,
> And of the holy londe
> Of Irlande.
>
> Gode sire, pray ich thee,
> For of sainte charite,
> Come and daunce wit me
> In Irlaunde.

The speaker in this poem (No. 31 in Davies) is evidently a woman; but she is not the betrayed maiden of the *chanson de femme*. Instead of complaint, she utters a mysterious invitation. Who is this Irish woman who prays men to come and dance with her in Ireland? A partial answer is suggested, perhaps, by the form of the poem, which appears to be a carol, like the Jankin poem and 'Now Springes the Spray'. As R. L. Greene shows in *The Early English Carols*, the term 'carol', when applied to the Middle English lyric, means 'a song on any subject, composed of uniform stanzas and provided with a burden'.[7] This form is originally associated with round dances, where the leader would sing the stanzas and the rest of the dancers reply with the refrain in chorus. 'Ich am of Irlaunde' is preserved on a strip of parchment together with other poems (including the well-known 'Maiden in the Mor Lay', Davies No. 33) almost all of which seem to be dance-songs, or at least songs; and if we imagine it performed by carollers, as Greene suggests it was, it begins to make some sense. For the dancers themselves it may have been enough to identify 'Ireland', in the make-believe geography of the dance floor, with the area occupied by the soloist at the centre of the ring of carollers. The symbolism of dance might then serve to explain why this area should be a 'holy land' ('Weave a circle round him thrice'). Yet the poem remains mysterious. Perhaps, unlike the great majority of Middle English lyrics, it is a genuine folk song. In any case, it serves as a forceful reminder that not all these lyrics can be understood in terms of known genres and traditions.

II

The preceding section illustrated some of the workings of genre in Middle English literature with examples from drama and lyric; what follows will be concerned with some main genres of *narrative* poetry. The main strength of English literature in this period—as in Old English—lies in narrative, rather than in lyric or dramatic writing. This is indeed the period within which English narrative verse reaches its apogee, in the Ricardian age, with the work of the *Gawain*-poet, Gower, and Chaucer; and throughout the period narrative proliferates in a rich variety of forms, prose and verse. The variety defies summary. 'Narrative' is itself a broad category; and the main divisions of narrative recognized in modern times—fiction, history, biography, and the rest—can be made out only imperfectly in medieval writings. In particular, the distinction between fiction and non-fiction, so fundamental to the modern system of genres, was relatively little regarded. The range of narrative writing in Middle English may be better suggested if we override the distinction between fact and fiction, and concentrate first on more formal criteria of *scope* and *scale*.

The world of people and events, real and imaginary, is infinite; and all narratives define, in one way or another, their own chosen limitations. Among other things, this means defining their 'scope': how much they intend to include, that is, and upon what general principle of selection. Like other aspects of narrative, 'scope' is governed by conventions which enable the reader to discover as soon as possible what he is to expect. The reader of Middle English narrative soon comes to recognize three main kinds, or rather degrees, of scope. Modern terminology is unsatisfactory, because our words almost all carry unwanted implications of factuality or fictionality; and I can do no better than christen the three sorts of narrative 'Histories', 'Lives', and 'Tales', intending the terms to signify progressively narrower kinds of scope.

The two best-known Histories in Middle English are Laȝamon's *Brut* and Malory's *Morte d'Arthur*. Laȝamon's poem takes as its subject the whole history of the Kings of Britain, starting with Brutus, the legendary founder of the dynasty, and ending with Cadwallader, the last of the British monarchs, under whom the British finally lost the kingdom to the English. Malory's work is comprehensive in a rather different fashion. He takes the reign of King Arthur (to which Laȝamon also devoted much space) and narrates, it would seem, all the stories of Arthur and his knights that he could find. The familiar title, apparently bestowed by William Caxton when he printed the book, is misleading: Malory's subject is not the death of Arthur, but the whole history of Arthur and the Round Table, starting with the strange circumstances of the king's birth. *Morte d'Arthur* and the *Brut* represent two roughly distinguishable principles of selection in Histories. One way is for the author to follow a topic chronologically, as Laȝamon follows the history of the Kings of Britain, producing a linear sequence of stories strung out in order of time on the thread of the topic. Another capital example of this type is *Cursor Mundi*, that huge poem which follows the history of man's salvation through all the seven ages of the world from Creation to Doomsday. The other type, which may be thought of as bunched rather than strung out, deals comprehensively with a single complex of events. This complex may be defined by a king's reign, as in Malory. Another favourite topic for a History was a siege. In Middle English verse there is a Siege of Milan, a Siege of Thebes, a Siege of Jerusalem, and a Siege of Troy. Thus the *Gest Historiale of the Destruction of Troy*, a long poem in correct and often spirited alliterative verse, deals comprehensively with the origins, course, and outcome of that most famous and protracted of sieges.

Histories such as these resist by their very comprehensiveness many of the demands which we commonly make on literary texts. Their numerous episodes, bunched or strung out, introduce many characters, some of them mere names and some conspicuous, but none attaining the status of protagonist or hero—not even Lancelot in *Morte d'Arthur*. Sometimes we may catch sight of some thematic principle of unity in the whole; but there will always be episodes, often baldly factual in character, which evidently owe their place simply to the arbitrary realities of history. Such and such a king reigned, such and such a battle took place, so the narrator reports it. History, said Aristotle, deals with 'the thing that has been', whereas poetry deals with 'the kind of thing that might be'. Yet, in classifying these works as 'histories', we must recognize, not merely that many of the events they report never actually took place, but also that the History is itself a literary phenomenon. There are formal parallels of a sort between Thomas Mann's *Buddenbrooks* and Laȝamon's *Brut*, and between the *Gest Historiale of the Destruction of Troy* and Tolstoy's *War and Peace*; but a modern parallel might better be drawn with the narratives of alternative worlds to be found in fantasy, science fiction, and children's literature. These often display (though in an explicitly fictional form) the same loose, comprehensive, polycentric narrative structure characteristic of medieval Histories. Perhaps the great success of J. R. R. Tolkien's *Lord of the Rings*—unaccountable as it seems to some readers—owes something to the fact that the book satisfies an appetite for large-scope narrative which novels generally fail to acknowledge. Tolkien (himself a distinguished medievalist) even finds room for genealogies, in which strung-out history is reduced to its barest essentials. In general, however, comprehensive narratives of this wide scope play little part in the canon of modern literature.

Turning to the second of the three main degrees of scope, we find something more congenial to current tastes. Like Histories, Lives deal with a number of episodes, often rather loosely strung out in chronological order; but they have a single protagonist, the subject of the Life, and he ensures a certain elementary unity at least. There are in Middle English two main types of Life: the *Vita Sancti* or Saint's Life,[8] and the Life of the chivalric hero. These have much in common; and it is not surprising to find the romance of Havelok recorded, under the title 'Vita Havelok', in a manuscript devoted chiefly to Saints' Lives. Romances, in fact, commonly keep company in the chief manuscript collections (e.g. the Lincoln Thornton Manuscript) with hagiographical and other pious pieces. Lives of saints and knights are both equally remote from the Life of the picaresque or low hero, a type altogether unrepresented in this period. Both deal with exemplary lives, marvellous events, and heroic deaths. Of the chivalric Lives, the most popular in late medieval England were evidently *Guy of Warwick* and *Beves of Hampton*, both originally written in French and translated into English and other languages. Chaucer refers to them together in *Sir Thopas*:

> Men speken of romances of prys,
> Of Horn child and of Ypotys,
> Of Beves and sir Gy.   (*Canterbury Tales* VII 897–9)

The basic principle of selection in such 'romances of prys' is simple: to report the adventures of a hero from cradle to grave, often, as in *Guy of Warwick*, with rambling and inconsequent results. Saints' Lives tend to be better constructed, partly because the genre had a longer history, going back in Latin to such models as the Life of St Martin by Sulpicius Severus (fourth century), and partly because the life of many saints has a natural climax in the *passio* or martyrdom. Such Lives are very common in Middle English, both in prose and verse. Among the earliest are the three prose lives of the virgin martyrs, Katherine, Juliana, and Margaret, composed at about the same period (*c*.1200) and in the same western dialect as *Ancrene*

Wisse. The best of all Middle English Saints' Lives, however, is Chaucer's *Second Nun's Tale*, which tells the life of St Cecilia. The mild, fluorescent beauty of this poem has suffered by comparison with other, more lively Canterbury tales. It is a minor masterpiece in a genre no longer congenial to most readers.

My third term, Tale, is meant to suggest the kind of narrative which deals with a single episode or with a single relatively close-knit series of episodes. Histories and Lives were often, as a matter of fact, created by combining a number of such Tales together. The ballad *Gest of Robyn Hode*, which almost amounts to a life of the greenwood hero, seems to have developed in this way out of a number of ballad Tales, as did the French Vulgate history of Arthur out of episodic romances.[9] Such compilations are common in the Middle Ages. Yet the distinction between the scope of the Tale and the broader scope of the Life remains quite clearly marked, for instance, in the literature of the saints, where the complete life or *Vita* contrasts with the *Passio*, which deals with the martyrdom, and with the *Miraculum*. A highly wrought instance of the latter genre in English is *St Erkenwald*, an alliterative poem of the Ricardian period, thought by some to be the work of the *Gawain*-poet, but probably by another anonymous poet. This remarkable work concentrates on a single miraculous episode in the life of the saint: the discovery of the body of a just judge marvellously preserved in its tomb since pagan times, and the disintegration of the body once the saint has baptized it with a falling tear. The poem packs much vivid narrative detail into its 352 lines, but all of it is selected for its bearing on the chosen story. Another *Miraculum*, Chaucer's *Prioress's Tale*, displays a similar richness of detail controlled by an equally strict sense of relevance. The story here is not a saint's miracle but a miracle of the Virgin—a genre which originated in England in the early twelfth century and remained popular there throughout the Middle Ages.[10] The whole of Chaucer's tale is directed towards the moment when the body of the murdered boy reveals its whereabouts by singing a favourite anthem in praise of Mary; and it is this miracle which impresses the pilgrims:

> Whan seyd was al this miracle, every man
> As sobre was that wonder was to se.

(Canterbury Tales VII 691–2)

This formal contrast in religious narrative between the *Miraculum* and the *Vita* is matched in secular romance by the contrast between chivalric Lives and those romances which concentrate on a single episode—a love story or an adventure. Unlike the literature of the saints, medieval romance had no learned Latin tradition behind it.[11] The term 'romance' itself has no clear generic meaning in Middle English (or, some would say, in Modern

English either); and the contemporary terminology for distinguishing its varieties was not adequate. The word 'lay', however, was sometimes used in Middle English to distinguish romance Tales from Lives or Histories. The *Gawain*-poet uses the term in this sense (to be distinguished from its other sense, 'a song accompanied by a stringed instrument') when he introduces his poem with these words:

> If ye wyl lysten this laye bot on littel quile,
> I schal telle hit as-tit, as I in toun herde. (30–1)

> If you will listen to this lay for just a little while, I shall tell it immediately, as I heard it in town.

Certainly *Sir Gawain* observes the limits of its chosen scope with extreme deliberation. It tells the story of a single, though complex, adventure—the Adventure of the Green Chapel—selected from among the 'wonders of Arthur' (29). Some modern critics have attempted to interpret the story as part of the Life of its hero, or even as part of the whole History of the Round Table; but the poem seems to resist such readings. Gawain's general reputation as a philanderer finds no place in it, and the tragedy of Arthur does not impend. The poet's knowledge of the Arthurian world is never in question—he knew the French Vulgate Cycle—but he excludes almost everything which is not relevant to the 'chaunce of the grene chapel' (2399).

A preference for the narrow-scope Tale over the extended Life or massive History is characteristic of the best works of the Ricardian period. Chaucer's *Troilus* is an outstanding example:

> The double sorwe of Troilus to tellen,
> That was the kyng Priamus sone of Troye,
> In lovynge, how his aventures fellen
> Fro wo to wele, and after out of joie,
> My purpos is . . . (I 1–5)

Chaucer makes his purposes plain in these opening lines. His subject is the story of Troilus's tragic love, not the life of the hero or the history of the siege of Troy; and throughout his poem, for all its length and incomparable richness of detail, he adheres to this subject, treating Troilus's feats of arms only in passing. As he says, he leaves aside 'things collateral' (I 262) and avoids digressions (I 143). Such deliberate narrowing of scope brings with it certain advantages, fully appreciated by most readers today. Because they concentrate on a single episode or sequence, Tales often exhibit a more fully developed significance than Lives or Histories. Thematically they are easier to control. In a lay like *Sir Gawain*, this control is almost complete. The poet's command of the art of exemplification enables him to integrate story and theme so thoroughly that the narrative has virtually none of those arbitrary and insignificant moments which seem inevitable in works of larger scope.

The other advantage of small-scope narrative will appear if we turn to consider the second of the two formal criteria: scale. Whereas scope concerns the amount and complexity of narrative material, scale concerns the degree of detail with which that material is presented.[12] If all narratives were the same length, it might be true to say that scope and scale vary inversely, as in a map of standard size (the larger the scale, the less country covered); but narratives vary in length, and in any case they are not committed, as maps are, to any overall consistency of scale. Scale will vary from part to part. Indeed, control of that variation is one of the essential arts of story-telling. Nevertheless, there must in general be more opportunity for large-scale (detailed or close-up) narrative in Tales than in Lives or Histories, simply because there is less story to tell. They can therefore more easily be told 'in a lenger wise', as Chaucer puts it (*Canterbury Tales* VII 2459).

Medieval rhetoricians treat what I have called 'scale' in a matter-of-fact and impartial fashion. Geoffrey of Vinsauf says that a writer may take either one of two roads: either to 'treat the matter with brevity' or to 'draw it out at length' (*Poetria Nova* 206–10).[13] Amplification and abbreviation are both legitimate procedures of art. Modern readers, on the other hand, have a strong, though often unacknowledged, predilection for large-scale story-telling, derived from their experience of novels and films. Largeness of scale is one of the prime conditions of that realistic effect which most people still look for in stories—and fail to find in the summary, chronicling manner of much medieval narrative. *Troilus* and *Sir Gawain* both make a strong appeal to this taste. Both authors, indeed, seem to have been independently experimenting with a scale of narrative larger than any previously attempted in Middle English. Chaucer obliquely acknowledges this in an interesting passage:

> But now, paraunter, som man wayten wolde
> That every word, or soonde, or look, or cheere
> Of Troilus that I rehercen sholde,
> In al this while unto his lady deere.
> I trowe it were a long thyng for to here;
> Or of what wight that stant in swich disjoynte,
> His wordes alle, or every look, to poynte.
>
> For sothe, I have naught herd it don er this
> In story non, ne no man here, I wene.   (III 491–9)

paraunter] perhaps   *soonde*] message   *cheere*] expression   *Or . . .
disjoynte*] or of any man who finds himself in such a predicament   *poynte*]
describe   *wene*] think

Obviously the ideal of total narrative ('*every* word . . .') is unattainable, as
Chaucer says; but one can read a claim into his disclaimer—a claim to have
gone further than his predecessors, and perhaps as far as good sense
allows, towards that inconceivable goal, in 'pointing' the words and looks
of his characters. Chaucer here uses the word 'point' in a rare, technical
sense, 'describe in detail'. The only other instance of this usage recorded in
Middle English comes in *Sir Gawain*, in a similar passage of disclaimer:

> for to telle therof hit me tene were,
> And to poynte hit yet I pyned me paraventure.   (1008–9)

> It would be difficult for me to tell of it, even if perhaps I took pains to describe
> it in detail.

Sir Gawain and *Troilus* provide many instances of how Tales may be
enriched by detailed pointing. Since Chaucer twice mentions 'looks' in the
passage just quoted, we may illustrate this large-scale narrative method
with some examples of the way Chaucer and the *Gawain*-poet render that
particular sort of detail. Looks (glances, glares, stares, ogles, and the rest)
play an important part in Chaucer's poetry from the beginning of his career
(e.g. *Book of the Duchess* 862–77); and in *Troilus* it is Criseyde's look which
first captivates the hero:

> To Troilus right wonder wel with alle
> Gan for to like hire mevynge and hire chere,
> Which somdel deignous was, for she let falle
> Hire look a lite aside in swich manere,
> Ascaunces, 'What! may I nat stonden here?'
> And after that hir lokynge gan she lighte,
> That nevere thoughte hym seen so good a syghte.   (I 288–94)

> *like*] appeal   *chere*] expression   *somdel deignous*] somewhat haughty
> *Ascaunces*] as if to say   *lighte*] lighten

Like the courtly mistress of 'Your Eyen Two', Criseyde both arouses
trepidation, by her scornful glance, and also offers some reassurance,
when she 'lightens' her look. But she is more than the stereotyped sweet
foe of courtly love literature. Her scornful look had about it a certain
hesitancy ('*somdel* deignous'). She did not gaze defiantly about, but 'let
falle hire look a lite aside': it is a downward look, evidently, and one which
claims, by its slight deviation from the perpendicular ('*a lite* aside'), no
more than a modest amount of standing space in the crowded temple of

Palladion. Yet Chaucer's reading of the look is firm enough (it was if she said 'What! may I nat stonden here?'); and he suggests considerable self-command—even a touch of the calculating—when he says that Criseyde 'let fall' and 'lightened' her looks. The total effect is not so much morally ambiguous as delectably mysterious.

Criseyde's look shows narrative scale to be more than a merely technical matter. To 'point' such a look is to invest it with significance. Herein lies the reason why large-scale narrative in Middle English tends to be sophisticated or courtly in character. The popular romancers waste little time on the minutiae of social life because they see no significance in 'every word, or soonde, or look, or cheere'. It is gentlemen and moralists who may see the importance of such things: for them, the details matter. One could compile an anthology of looks from *Sir Gawain* which would illustrate this: the Green Knight looking straight over the heads of Arthur and his knights as he delivers his challenge ('heghe he over loked' 223); Arthur glancing at Gawain as he makes his uneasy joke about the axe ('he glent upon Sir Gawen' 476); the lady peeping in at Gawain as he lies in bed ('at the knyght totes' 1476) and shooting him secret glances of amorous complicity at supper ('stille stollen countenaunce' 1659); Gawain looking with exaggerated horror at the boar's head to flatter its conqueror ('let lodly therat the lorde for to here' 1634) and squinting up at the axe as it falls ('glyfte hym bysyde' 2265). Few passages illustrate better the virtues of large-scale narrative than that which describes how the lady first visits Gawain's bedroom (1182–1203). A small-scale version might run as follows: 'And the next morning the beautiful lady of the castle came secretly to his chamber and . . .' Instead the *Gawain*-poet points the episode, with a particularly effective notation of looks. When Gawain first hears his door move, he lifts his head out of the bedclothes, draws aside a corner of the bedcurtain, and takes a cautious look. What he sees makes him drop down and pretend to be asleep; and it is only when the lady has sat waiting on his bed for some time that he decides he had better wake up:

> Then he wakenede, and wroth, and to hir warde torned,
> And unlouked his ye-lyddez, and let as hym wondered.

> Then he woke up, and stretched, and turned towards her, and unlocked his eyelids, and behaved as if he was astonished.

'Unlocked his eyelids' is particularly good. Alliterative verse tends to make all physical actions sound heavy and deliberate; but here the heaviness and deliberation is dramatically right. Gawain really does, reluctantly and with conscious effort, unlock his eyelids.

Gawain and *Troilus* are capital examples of Tales—an adventure and a love-story—treated at length as large-scale, free-standing narratives.

There was, however, another way of treating Tales, and also Lives: to bring a number of them together into a collection. Unlike free-standing narratives, such compilations occur more often in medieval than in modern literature. They may be regarded as the literary equivalents of the great Summas produced by the lawyers and theologians of the age, testifying to the same urge to compile and order scattered materials into comprehensive wholes. Scribes often produced such collections simply by their grouping of texts (the collection of romances in the Lincoln Thornton Manuscript, for instance); but modern readers normally meet collections of this simple kind only when the constituents are held by the editor to have been originally written or planned as a single whole. This is the case, for instance, with the *South English Legendary*, a large compilation of Saints' Lives, first assembled in the thirteenth century, probably at Gloucester. Robert Henryson's remarkable *Moral Fables of Aesop* is a collection of the same type, though this is clearly the work of a single author, unlike the *Legendary*, and Henryson makes sporadic attempts to relate the individual tales, by linking some of them together and providing a general prologue.

Other Middle English collections of Tales exhibit a more complex organization, in which the Tales are embedded in a setting and related together thematically and also, sometimes, dramatically. Robert Mannyng of Brunne's *Handlyng Synne*, for instance, takes the form of a treatise on the sacrament of penance; but its various divisions—on the Ten Commandments, the Seven Deadly Sins, and so on—are so richly illustrated with stories that the work might also be regarded as a collection of Tales thematically arranged. The same can be said with more certainty of Gower's *Confessio Amantis*, in which a scheme very like Mannyng's is dramatized and partially secularized. As in *Handlyng Synne*, Gower's stories are introduced as illustrations—illustrative *exempla* of the Seven Deadly Sins—to help a right confession; but in this case they are put in the mouth of a Confessor, Genius, addressing a penitent, Amans, whose confessions themselves form part of the poem's fiction. This Lover's Confession provides a setting much more lively and sophisticated than Mannyng's for the constituent Tales; but Gower's thematic framework is just as rigid as his predecessor's: Genius goes through the sins in turn, illustrating each with stories. It is only in the *Canterbury Tales* that we find the dramatic playing a more important part than the thematic principle in organizing a collection of Tales.

In the most of these collections, distinctions of genre play little part, either because the constituent Tales all belong to the same genre (saints' legend in the *Legendary*, animal fable in the *Fables*), or because, where in more complex collections the thematic principle prevails, the didactic purpose tends to neutralize generic differences: all the stories in *Handlyng*

Synne and *Confessio Amantis* function in the same way, as *exempla*. By contrast, the plan of Chaucer's *Canterbury Tales* throws the characteristics of the different genres into bold relief. Even in its unfinished state, the work displays at least one clear example of most of the main types of Tale current in Middle English. It therefore provides a good basis for some further reflections on the significance of genre in this period.

The *Canterbury Tales* is an unfinished work, and the order of its parts presents many difficult problems; but it is at least clear that Chaucer intended to begin the story-telling on the road to Canterbury with the *Knight's Tale* and to follow that with the *Miller's Tale*. By starting with these two stories, the poet declares at the outset his interest in variety and contrast—the way stories differ from each other. Both the Knight and the Miller begin with the same story-teller's word 'whilom' (like 'once upon a time', but without the nursery flavour); but after that first word their stories set off in completely different directions. Here is the Knight:

> Whilom, as olde stories tellen us,
> Ther was a duc that highte Theseus;
> Of Atthenes he was lord and governour.   (I 859–61)
>
> *highte*] was called

And here is the Miller:

> Whilom ther was dwellynge at Oxenford
> A riche gnof, that gestes heeld to bord,
> And of his craft he was a carpenter   (I 3187–9)
>
> *gnof*] fellow   *heeld to bord*] had as lodgers

The Knight's 'whilom', supported by a reference to 'olde stories', means what it says: his Tale is set in the remote past. The Miller's 'whilom', on the other hand, turns out to be a mere formality: his Tale belongs to the present. This difference in time is matched by a difference in space: Oxford as against Athens. The Miller's 'riche gnof', too, belongs to a different social world from the Knight's 'duc': on the one hand, an Oxford carpenter, wealthy but coarse ('gnof' has churlish associations), who takes in student lodgers; on the other, Duke Theseus, lord and governor of Athens. The contrast between these two persons is pointed as the plots unfold by an absurd parellelism between their roles. Theseus and John the Carpenter both play the part of keeper to the heroine. The two young Theban knights, Palamon and Arcite, compete for the beautiful Amazonian maid Emily, whose hand in marriage is in the gift of her brother-in-law Theseus; and two young Oxford gallants, the student Nicholas and the parish clerk Absolon, compete for the pretty Alison, who is jealously guarded by her old husband John. There is a general parallel between the two plots, serving to emphasize the differences between them. Palamon and Arcite compete for the object of their romantic passion by long service and feats of knightly arms; but Nicholas wins Alison by playing a comic trick on her husband, and discomforts his rival Absolon with a crude insult.

What is the significance of these contrasts? Most readers, I think, interpret them in a realistic, even a sociological fashion. Unlike that other great fourteenth-century collection of Tales, Boccaccio's *Decameron*, the *Canterbury Tales* assembles a body of story-tellers which is socially very varied—from the Knight, the Squire, the Franklin, and the Monk, down to the Miller, the Cook, the Plowman, and the Summoner. We tend, therefore, to relate the variety of the Tales to the social variety of the tellers, as if Chaucer were recording what sorts of tale different sorts of people were likely to know and tell. This is an impression which Chaucer does something to encourage. Knights did not normally compose or recite romances; but it is natural to suppose that stories of chivalry would appeal specially to the 'gentils', as indeed the *Knight's Tale* does (*Canterbury Tales* I 3113). A taste for funny stories of sex and trickery seems equally appropriate to the Miller, described in the *General Prologue* as 'a janglere and a goliardeys'. Chaucer creates such a powerful illusion of reality, in fact, that the reader is tempted to take his fiction as a literal report, as if he could derive from it a true picture of the distribution of literary genres among the various classes of fourteenth-century society. We know that the *Knight's Tale* is a romance, and we are told that the *Miller's Tale* is a fabliau. Does it not then follow, from the evidence Chaucer provides, that fabliau belonged to the literature of the populace, just as romance belonged to the literature of the courtly classes? But within the fictional world of the Canterbury pilgrimage what the Knight tells is a tale of chivalry, not a romance, and what the Miller tells is a tale of 'synne and harlotries', not a literary fabliau. The distinction seems niggling; but it is crucial, at least in the case of fabliau.

The term 'fabliau' belongs in the first place to a genre of French poetry which developed towards the end of the twelfth century and flourished especially in the thirteenth.[14] Fabliaux were short narrative poems in the same octosyllabic couplet which was standard in the French verse romances of the time. They generally tell stories of trickery, by which characters win money or goods or sexual favours, or all three, from stooges and victims. The fabliau-writers evidently derived these cynical but often ingenious tales mostly from the popular stock of funny stories (known as Merry Tales to students of folklore), and they tended to give them popular, everyday settings. The nature of these stories and their settings led the French medievalist Joseph Bédier, in his study *Les Fabliaux* (1893), to see the fabliau as a 'bourgeois genre', belonging to what he called 'la poésie des carrefours' (the poetry of the crossroads) as against 'la poésie des chateaux'—the courtly romances of Chrétien de Troyes, for instance. Fabliaux, according to Bédier, were written for non-courtly audiences and expressed, in their portrayal of popular life, 'bourgeois' values which stood in deliberate opposition to the fanciful idealisms of romance. However, in a later study, also called *Les Fabliaux*, published in 1957, Per Nykrog argued convincingly that Bédier was wrong to identify these poems, historically, with the social world which they portray. He showed that the taste for fabliaux was by no means confined to popular audiences. Maybe he goes too far in the opposite direction when he describes fabliau as a '*courtly* burlesque genre'; but he is surely right to insist that the distinctive characteristics of fabliau are best understood, not as manifestations of bourgeois realism, but as features of a literary genre. For medieval poets, Nykrog remarks, 'the distinction between genres is at bottom a social distinction'. The modest social settings, accordingly, should not be taken as defining the class of audience for which these poets wrote. It is rather the appropriate setting for this sort of poem, just as are certain kinds of character and certain kinds of sentiment. This doctrine of decorum can be found formally stated in medieval Latin treatises. The diagram known as 'Virgil's wheel' took Virgil's *Eclogues*, *Georgics*, and *Aeneid* as representing the three levels of style (*humilis*, *mediocris*, and *gravis*), and specified for each the appropriate type of character, proper name, animal, instrument, setting, and tree. Thus the cedar is a high-style tree (as in *Troilus* II 918).[15] But the basic idea hardly requires documentation from learned sources. Modern audiences still tend to associate comedy with low life, despite the challenge presented by low-life tragedies such as Arthur Miller's *Death of a Salesman*.

The surviving evidence suggests that English writers, so ready to imitate French romance, took little interest in fabliau; and by the later fourteenth century the genre was no longer alive in the country of its birth. It is therefore surprising that Chaucer should have taken it up. No other genre, indeed, is better represented among the *Canterbury Tales*. As well as the *Miller's Tale*, the Tales of the Reeve and the Shipman are clearly modelled on the French type; so too, though not so clearly, are the Tales of the Merchant and the Summoner. The fragmentary *Cook's Tale* also starts, quite brilliantly, in the fabliau way. The list of pilgrims selected by Chaucer to tell this kind of tale—Miller, Reeve, Shipman, Merchant, Summoner, Cook—seems at first sight to support Bédier's conception of fabliau as 'la poésie des carrefours'; but there is a better explanation. The Canterbury pilgrimage is itself a poetic fiction; and the same principle of poetic decorum which required a certain sort of character to *people* the fabliau would also have dictated the sort of character to *tell* them. The two sets of characters, in Chaucer's poem, have much in common. The pilgrim Miller could easily have appeared in a fabliau himself. Indeed he more or less does just that, in the following tale told by the Reeve. For the latter, having taken offence at something in the Miller's story, incorporates him, in an unmistakable portrait, into his own fabliau story—an environment into which the Miller fits perfectly. Similarly the merchant in the *Shipman's Tale* is quite like the Merchant who tells the *Merchant's Tale*. All six fabliau-tellers, in fact, could easily go into fabliau tales themselves. This is not because they are all bourgeois (they are not, unless one misuses the term), but rather because they all belong to occupations which provided special opportunities for the kind of trickery which is the stuff of fabliau comedy: the Miller in his dealings with customers (*General Prologue*, I 562), the Reeve with his lord (I 610–12), the Shipman with his merchant hirers (I 396–7), the Merchant with business associates (I 279–80), the Summoner with offenders (I 649–50), and the Cook with diners (*Cook's Prologue*, I 4346–8). They are all, in their different ways, middlemen (which is not the same as being middle-class) and enjoy the opportunities of that position.

By attributing his fabliau tales to pilgrims who might have figured in them, Chaucer blurs the distinction between the fiction of the pilgrimage and the fictions which it encloses. Identical principles of literary decorum govern both. Yet at the same time he insists that the pilgrimage, unlike the events related by the pilgrims in their tales, really happened. The result is one of those rich confusions that Chaucer loved to explore. His apology before the *Miller's Tale* shows him at work:

> What sholde I moore seyn, but this Millere
> He nolde his wordes for no man forbere,
> But tolde his cherles tale in his manere.
> M'athynketh that I shal reherce it heere.
> And therfore every gentil wight I preye,
> For Goddes love, demeth nat that I seye
> Of yvel entente, but for I moot reherce
> Hir tales alle, be they bettre or werse,
> Or elles falsen som of my mateere.
> And therfore, whoso list it nat yheere,
> Turne over the leef and chese another tale.   (I 3167–77)

nolde] would not *forbere*] restrain *M'athynketh*] I regret *shal reherce*] must repeat *falsen*] misrepresent *list*] wishes

This is transparently an unreal excuse—the pilgrimage was not a historical event, nor was Chaucer obliged to report it—but it is no more unreal than the offence for which it is offered. The tone makes it clear that Chaucer did not for a moment expect 'gentil wights' to take offence at his fabliaux, still less to skip them. The underlying assumption seems to be that polite readers would be perfectly familiar with such things, and would leave silly scruples to 'low minds' (as someone says in the *Decameron*). Such readers could be trusted to understand and enjoy the logic of a comic genre, just as the lord and lady at the end of the *Summoner's Tale* receive with amused equanimity the friar's scandalized report of the churl's fart: 'a cherl hath doon a cherles dede' (III 2206). As Chaucer himself says at the end of his apology for the Miller: 'men shal nat maken ernest of game'.

Romance and fabliau represent, in the system of vernacular genres established by French poets in the twelfth century, the two opposite extremes of secular narrative. In the *Canterbury Tales*, the Tales of Knight and Miller, standing in bold opposition at the beginning of the work, establish the two poles of its secular story-telling. Five of the ensuing tales, as has already been noticed, belong to the lower hemisphere, at or near the fabliau pole; and four other tales, we may now add, belong to the upper hemisphere, at or near the romance pole. The *Squire's Tale*—unfinished, and now unjustly neglected—represents a type of romance more youthful and extravagant than that of his father, the Knight. In the tale of the Wife of Bath, who unexpectedly provides Chaucer's only Arthurian story, romance shades off into fairy tale. Chaucer's own *Sir Thopas* burlesques the absurdities of popular English minstrel romance. The Franklin announces his tale as a Breton lay:

> Thise olde gentil Britouns in hir dayes
> Of diverse aventures maden layes,
> Rymeyed in hir firste Briton tonge.   (V 709–11)

The Breton lay is one of the best documented of all medieval narrative genres. Its remoter origins lie, as Chaucer knew, in Brittany; but it was a French poet, Marie de France, in the great creative period of the twelfth century, who established the genre in its regular medieval form: a short romance, usually in octosyllabic couplets, dealing with a single 'aventure'.[16] Because Marie drew upon the narrative repertoire of the Breton minstrels, the stories—mostly romantic love stories—were coloured by the Celtic passion for magic and faerie. In the work of her followers, this feature seems to have established itself as a characteristic of the genre. The Middle English lay *Sir Orfeo* shows how even a Classical story was reworked, either by the English poet or by a French predecessor, into conformity with this tradition. Whereas the Classical Eurydice was bitten by a snake, the medieval Heurodys is carried off by the fairy; and

Orfeo's journey takes him not to Hades but to a land of fairy which exhibits certain Celtic features. In Chaucer's *Franklin's Tale*, however, this characteristic appears somewhat weakened. The story of Dorigen's dilemma turns on a marvel—the disappearance of the rocks from round the coast of Brittany—but Chaucer partially rationalizes the marvel by tracing it to the 'natural magic' of a scholar of Orleans, whose book-learning enables him to produce such illusions. Just so in *Sir Gawain and the Green Knight*— also, it will be recalled, announced as a 'lay'—the marvel of the Green Knight is traced back, via Morgan le Fay, to the book-learning of Merlin. Yet *Sir Gawain*, like the *Franklin's Tale*, testifies to the continuing strength of romance traditions in late fourteenth-century England.

The distinction between secular and religious cannot always be clearly drawn, even in the *Canterbury Tales*; but it is possible to make out there a set of ecclesiastical narrative genres distinct from, and to some degree parallel with, the secular set. In this case the hierarchy is topped by the two genres already mentioned: the Saint's Life and the Miracle of the Virgin. Chaucer assigns these to the Prioress and her chaplain, the Second Nun. Both nuns mark the elevated character of their Tales with formal prologues, each incorporating the invocation to the Virgin with which Miracles and Saints' Lives customarily opened. Few other Canterbury Tales start with prologues (as distinct from being preceded by one); and the only prologue which matches the formal elevation of the two nuns is the Man of Law's: 'O hateful harm, condicion of poverte!' Generically the *Man of Law's Tale* may seem something of a puzzle. It has undoubted affinities with the romance tales; but its protagonist, Constance, is reduced by her character and sex to a state of passivity so complete that she seems more like a saint than a heroine of romance—a 'hooly creature', as the Man of Law himself calls her (II 1149). In this, Constance resembles Griselda in the *Clerk's Tale*. We should regard both Tales as falling into the no man's land between romance and saint's life. They testify to the affinity between the two genres—each at the head of its own generic hierarchy.

The two hierarchies, secular and religious, exhibit other less elevated affinities—notably, in the *Canterbury Tales*, between the fabliau and the *exemplum*. The latter term (Middle English 'ensample') refers in its most general sense to any anecdote or description introduced to illustrate or prove a point. Such formal examples occur in all sorts of medieval writing, but they are particularly associated with the sermon. In the thirteenth and fourteenth centuries especially preachers made liberal use of *exempla*; and treatises on the art of preaching (*de arte praedicatoria*) stress the value of illustrative stories and descriptions, particularly for unlearned audiences who, as one puts it, 'are more readily moved by tangible examples than by the citation of authorities or deep general truths'.[17] From the middle of the thirteenth century, friars and others gathered *exempla* together into great collections organized, sometimes alphabetically and sometimes thematically, for the benefit of writers looking for a suitable illustration to point a moral or adorn a sermon.

Exempla represent a way of thinking very widespread throughout Middle English literature, as we shall see in the next chapter; but the present subject is not 'exemplification' as a general mode of meaning, but the *exemplum* as a specific genre of narrative. The prime instance in the *Canterbury Tales* is the *Pardoner's Tale*. Here the relationship between tale and teller is as direct and literal as could be. Pardoners were notorious for their populist manner of preaching; and this particular pardoner, as he explains himself, regularly uses *exempla* to catch the attention of his audience:

> Thanne telle I hem ensamples many oon
> Of olde stories longe tyme agoon.
> For lewed peple loven tales olde;
> Swiche thynges kan they wel reporte and holde.   (VI 435–8)

He introduces his Tale as 'a moral tale . . . which I am wont to preche for to wynne'; and although its narrative scale goes beyond what would normally be possible in an actual sermon, the Tale is a true *exemplum*. The story of the three wild young men and their encounter with death specifically and explicitly illustrates the Pardoner's favourite theme, *Radix malorum est cupiditas*, by showing how avarice leads the three friends to kill each other. The fact that these friends remain unnamed marks the subordination of story to theme; and the denouement comes close, for all its chilling details, to abstract demonstration: while A goes to fetch provisions, B and C plan to kill him . . . Many *exempla* concern named persons, whose historical or legendary stories lend authority to the general truth they illustrate; but the nameless type, to which the *Pardoner's Tale* belongs, is equally characteristic of the genre. The very absence of names in such Tales claims for them an unrestricted relevance.

Another Chaucerian instance of this type is less well known: the *Friar's Tale*. Friars and pardoners were commonly regarded as rivals in the lucrative business of popular preaching, as in John Heywood's play *The Pardoner and the Friar* (printed 1533); and it would therefore have seemed natural that Chaucer should choose a preacher's *exemplum* for his Friar as well as for his Pardoner. A number of contemporary *exemplum* collections contain versions of the Friar's story, which concerns a summoner who was carried off by a devil after being heartily cursed by one of his victims; and, although the Friar's chief purpose is to ridicule the pilgrim Summoner, his story has much in common with the Pardoner's 'moral tale': a nameless protagonist ('a somonour'), an everyday setting in village and countryside, and a plot whose vigorous twists serve to drive home a moral point. At the same time, the *Friar's Tale* shows how hard it can sometimes be, among these lower genres, to distinguish religious from secular. The Friar's angry portrait of a summoner in his *exemplum* provokes the Summoner to respond in a fabliau with his hostile portrait of a friar; yet there is no more sense of generic contrast here than in the pair of fabliaux told by the quarrelling Miller and Reeve. *Exemplum* and fabliau, in fact, overlap at many points. Both often portray the same world of ordinary people, who are either nameless or, at best, marked by common names such as 'Thomas', 'John', or 'Alison'; and both favour plots which, unlike most plots of romances or saints' lives, end with a series of twists. It might be supposed that the moral intention of *exemplum* would set it apart from fabliau; but in fact a large number of French fabliaux (two-thirds, according to Nykrog) conclude with a moral generalization of some sort. This curious characteristic, which prompted Nykrog to speculate about historical connections between fabliau and *exemplum*, appears also in Chaucer. Three of the five completed fabliau tales prompt moral or prudential reflections from the pilgrims. The Cook, for instance, reacts to the *Reeve's Tale* exactly as if it were an improving *exemplum*:

> 'Wel seyde Salomon in his langage,
> "Ne bryng nat every man into thyn hous";
> For herberwynge by nyghte is perilous.
> Wel oghte a man avysed for to be
> Whom that he broghte into his pryvetee.'   (I 4330–4)

herberwynge] giving lodging   *pryvetee*] private dwelling

The lack of a clear distinction between fabliau and *exemplum* serves as a reminder (if any is needed) that the genres of Middle English literature are not to be regarded as a fixed set of sharply distinguished categories into which all texts can be comfortably fitted. The paucity and uncertainty of their genre-terminology is enough to suggest that the writers themselves would not have seen the matter that way. Yet one has only to recapitulate the various genres singled out in this chapter to see that, however blurred their boundaries, they do represent markedly different ways of making plays, lyrics, and stories. Mystery plays and morality plays; courtly love complaints, meditations on the Passion, *chansons de femme*, *chansons d'aventure*, and complaints of Christ; romances, lays, saint's lives, miracles of the Virgin, fabliaux, and *exempla*—they all have their own traditions and their own characteristics. No individual work of any merit, of course, can adequately be discussed simply in terms of the genre to which it belongs: criticism cannot rest content with the kinds of classification and description offered in this chapter. Nevertheless, the most sophisticated criticism of the most singular masterpieces must still keep generic distinctions in view. Chaucer's *Canterbury Tales* illustrates forcibly the determining power, then as now, of genre. Character, setting, plot, and style are all, in these Tales, varied according to generic principles. We have seen, too, how one and the same feature—a devil, a first-person pronoun, a nameless character—can function differently according to the genre in which it appears. So recognition of genre is not merely an academic exercise: it is an indispensable condition of understanding.

4 Modes of meaning

The matters discussed in the previous chapters have all been of a somewhat external or formal character: the nature of the Middle English period and its literature, the conditions under which texts were produced and received, and the importance of genre. These topics bear only indirectly on the meaning and value of individual works; but the meaning of individual works is not a matter that can be discussed in general terms. Attempts at wholesale interpretative criticism merely encourage the belief that all medieval works probably have more or less the *same* meaning. A book such as C. S. Lewis's *Discarded Image* performs a valuable service in so far as it explains the fundamental assumptions about God, man, and the universe which the Middle Ages inherited from Mediterranean antiquity, Semitic and Classical; but no one should suppose (Lewis certainly did not) that the meanings of individual texts can be derived directly from general knowledge of the Medieval World Picture. The literature of the Middle Ages is more consistent in its ideology than that of some other periods. The voice of religious scepticism, for instance, never speaks in Middle English literature. But medieval Christianity was a varied and eclectic faith; and the world picture which it promulgated allowed individuals a good deal of latitude, not least when writing poetry.

It would be undesirable, then, to attempt to predict the specific meanings that a reader will find in individual works such as *Troilus*, *Sir Gawain*, or *Piers Plowman*. Such works have their own specific intentions, which are easily distorted by introductory generalizations. This chapter, therefore, will confine itself to describing certain *kinds* of meaning to be encountered in Middle English—modes of meaning not familiar, in their medieval form, to most people today.

I

It is the *un*familiar modes of meaning which will require explanation; but I must begin by stressing that reading the literature of the Middle English period does not, as a general rule, require mastery of abstruse or special codes. It should not be supposed that there will always, or usually, turn out to be some mysterious medieval signification, if only one could find it, hidden beneath the surface of a text. Much Middle English writing is (linguistic difficulties apart) entirely plain and accessible. Where writers are expounding ideas, they employ arguments and allusions which are sometimes, inevitably, difficult for us to follow; but the difficulties usually arise from simple causes, most often from ignorance of the Bible. William Langland, for instance, knew the Psalms intimately—a Psalter was one of the tools of his trade, as he says (C V 45–7)—and he alludes to this book of the Bible especially often. Occasionally he expects the reader to recall the standard interpretation of a passage; but often the allusion is quite simple, and a reader who either knows the Psalm or is ready to look it up will find no difficulty. Even Langland—the most difficult, and also the most fascinating, of Middle English writers—generally expounds his thoughts in plain and direct language. English itself, one might say, was still in Langland's time a language which encouraged plainness and directness. High abstract thought had its own language: Latin.

Much non-expository writing is equally straightforward. Because narrative verse is such a rare and specialized form in modern times, we tend to look in it for intentions beyond those normally associated with telling a story. Why, after all, did the author produce a *poem*, instead of a novel, or a film, or a TV serial? But such an approach is obviously inappropriate, in general, to Middle English verse narrative, because verse had then little competition from more popular forms of story-telling. Many of the tail-rhyme and short-couplet romances, for instance, offer straightforward adventure stories of the rather fantastic sort associated in modern times with television or popular fiction. Such stories, of course, have their own kind of significance—but not of any abstrusely medieval character. *Havelok the Dane*, for instance, is not an allegory.

Allegory is one of the two less accessible modes of signification which I propose to discuss in this chapter. The other I shall refer to as 'exemplification', following medieval scholastic theorists, who called it 'modus exemplificativus'. These two modes often overlap in practice, but in theory there is a fundamental distinction between them. Exemplification treats facts or events (real or imagined) as examples which demonstrate some general truth; whereas allegory treats facts or events as metaphors which represent some truth or some other event. Allegory requires the reader to translate; exemplification requires him to generalize. These two closely related, and indeed sometimes almost indistinguishable, processes are fundamental to all reading: translation and generalization. The literature of every period presents the reader with images whose significance lies either in their representative value (literally taken), or in their suggestive resemblance to something else (taken metaphorically). We expect things

that happen in literature to be either symbolical, or typical, or both. That
is why they are significant. Allegory and exemplification should therefore
be regarded simply as manifestations—the most distinctively medieval
manifestations—of two modes of signification fundamental to all literature. What makes them different, and sometimes difficult to appreciate, is
their formal and explicit character—by comparison, that is, with most
recent manifestations of the same modes. When a story is a full *exemplum*,
like Chaucer's *Pardoner's Tale*, it will have stated in plain terms the general
truth which it is intended to demonstrate even before the narrative has
begun (as the Pardoner announces his theme: *Radix malorum est cupiditas*);
and the narrative itself should be pointed accordingly. The reader's freedom to generalize from the case is therefore restricted by the author, as it
would not normally be in a novel, from which we are most often left to
draw our own conclusions. Allegory differs from other less explicit kinds
of symbolical writing in a similar fashion. It tends to make its significations
explicit (by the use of allegorical names, most obviously), and also to
maintain and develop a single analogy in a relatively regular and sustained
way—whence the traditional rhetoricians' definition of allegory as '*extended* metaphor'. Allegory characteristically allows its reader less freedom
of interpretation than do other kinds of symbolism.

Many of the best works of the Middle English period articulate their
meanings in one or other of these relatively explicit modes: *Sawles Warde*,
The Owl and the Nightingale, *Confessio Amantis*, *Piers Plowman*, the *Pardoner's Tale*, *Patience*, Henryson's *Fables*, and many more. There can be
no question of confining the significance of such works to their explicit
meanings as allegories or *exempla*; but it is that explicit meaning, paradoxically, which requires most explanation and justification to the modern
reader. Let us begin with allegorical mode.[1]

The most comprehensive allegorical poem in Middle English is Langland's *Piers Plowman*. In the first dream of this multiple dream poem, after
the prologue, Langland presents two contrasting female figures called
Holy Church and Lady Meed; and the action of the poem begins with a
marriage proposed between the latter and a male character called Conscience. Personifications of this sort are to play a large part in *Piers*, as they
do in other Middle English works such as *Sawles Warde*, *Winner and
Waster*, Chaucer's *Parliament of Fowls*, Gower's *Confessio Amantis*, and the
morality plays. Personification is the most common form of what may be
called 'labelled' allegory, in which persons and also, less often, places and
things bear names which plainly indicate their significance—labels such as
Langland's 'Conscience' or Spenser's 'House of Pride'. This kind of
labelling is more or less confined today to cartoons and civic heraldry.
Elsewhere it will most often seem obtrusive and objectionable: a mere

'translation of abstract notions into a picture-language', as Coleridge said of allegory.[2] Whatever meanings are now looked for in literature, they are precisely *not* the sort of 'abstract notions' that can be conveyed by labels such as 'Conscience' or 'Pride'. The modern reader therefore finds it difficult to distinguish, amidst the naïve 'picture-language', things that labelled allegory does well. An example from Langland will make this clear.

In the middle section of *Piers Plowman* (from Passus VIII onwards, in the B Text), Langland devotes considerable time to a problem which evidently troubled him. How far are learning and intelligence necessary for that good Christian life which Langland calls 'Dowel'? What contribution do learned and clever men make to the Church? A long series of encounters between the dreamer Will and various personifications representing learning and intelligence (Wit, Thought, Study, Clergy, Scripture, Imaginatif) culminates at a dinner given by Conscience. In the discussion of Dowel which takes place at this dinner, the learned classes are represented at their worst by a glibly intellectual Friar; and even Learning himself ('Clergy') confesses himself stumped. The most impressive contribution to the symposium comes from a new arrival, the poor pilgrim Patience, who makes an obscure but impassioned speech about love (XIII 136–71). This repels the Friar by its idealism and Clergy by its cloudiness; but it fires Conscience, who determines to set out there and then on pilgrimage with Patience. Langland seems at this point to have come down at last on the side of evangelical fervour and simplicity, and against the learned establishment of the Church; but the end of the scene, where Conscience takes leave of his guests, brings the matter to a subtler conclusion. Conscience says a polite farewell to the Friar (there is no question of coming to terms with *him*), and then turns to murmur a parting message to Clergy:

'Me were levere, by Oure Lord, and I lyve sholde,
Have pacience parfitliche than half thi pak of bokes!'

(XIII 200–1)

Me were levere] I would rather   *and*] if

The crisply alliterated antithesis between patience and a 'pack' of books sounds purely dismissive; but there is a hint of compromise in preferring *perfect* patience to *half* a pack of books (one might have expected Conscience to prefer a little patience to the whole pack); and the exchange which follows suggests that perfection is in any case no simple matter:

Clergie of Conscience no congie wolde take,
But seide ful sobreliche, 'Thow shalt se the tyme
Whan thow art wery forwalked, wilne me to counseille.'

'That is sooth,' seide Conscience, 'so me God helpe!
If Pacience be oure partyng felawe and pryve with us bothe,
Ther nys wo in this world that we ne sholde amende,
And conformen kynges to pees, and alle kynnes londes—
Sarsens and Surre, and so forth alle the Jewes—
Turne into the trewe feith and intil oon bileve.'
'That is sooth,' quod Clergie, 'I se what thow menest.
I shall dwelle as I do, my devoir to shewe,
And confermen fauntekyns oother folk ylered
Til Pacience have preved thee and parfit thee maked.'   (202–14)
congie] leave   *Whan . . . counseille*] once you are exhausted with walking,
when you will be glad of my advice   *partyng felawe*] partner   *pryve*] intimate
conformen] dispose   *alle kynnes londes*] lands of every kind   *Sarsens and
Surre*] Saracens and Syria   *my devoir to shewe*] to do my public duty
confermen fauntekyns] confirm children   *ylered*] instructed

Conscience's farewell to Clergy represents, to all intents and purposes,
Langland's own farewell to the subject. He left it, on the evidence of this
soberly beautiful scene, with mixed feelings. The scene is dominated by
Conscience's ringing affirmation of universal faith and peace; but Clergy's
awareness of the difficulties involved does not seem merely pusillanimous.
Some day Conscience and Patience may indeed 'conformen kynges to
pees'; but in the meantime Clergy is surely right to fulfil his duties and
'confermen fauntekyns'. The verbal echo, from *conform* to *confirm*, draws
attention to Clergy's dry good sense. He speaks with the soberly realistic
voice of the Church establishment. Perhaps he does not believe that
Conscience will ever become 'parfit', and perhaps that is unworthy scepticism; but the poet allows him to speak with real dignity and weight.
Langland, in fact, divides the reader's sympathies (though not evenly)
between the two figures, and so expresses in allegorical fiction his own
divided response to the competing claims of evangelical enthusiasm and
the stored-up learning of the Church.

This lengthy analysis demonstrates a simple but fundamental point.
Allegories, whether labelled or not, require to be 'translated'; but the
first essential is to pay proper attention to the literal level of the story.
Interpreters of Scripture in the Middle Ages frequently insisted that sound
allegorical interpretation must rest upon a thorough understanding of the
prime, literal sense. St Thomas Aquinas said: 'All the senses are founded
on one, the literal, from which alone can any argument be drawn'; and St
Bonaventure: 'He who scorns the literal sense of Holy Scripture will never
rise to its spiritual meanings'.[3] The same principle should govern the
reading of non-scriptural allegory also. One cannot understand Langland's thoughts and feelings about the competing claims of enthusiasm and

learning without first truly seeing and hearing the scene which he has imagined between Clergy and Conscience.

Reading allegory, however, is not otherwise like reading a novel. Novel-readers expect meaning to emerge unobtrusively or 'naturally' from the world of the fiction; but in labelled allegory especially the meaning or *sententia* is made explicit within the fiction itself. The participants in Langland's dinner-scene are not merely taken to represent patience, conscience, and learning: they are *called* Patience, Conscience, and Learning. Such names mark them off as 'personifications'; and personifications are creatures of a fundamentally different kind from the characters in most novels. A figure bearing a name such as 'David Copperfield' purports to represent an individual human being; but a figure labelled 'Patience' represents one of the simpler constituents into which human behaviour can be analysed. It is therefore absurd to expect a personification itself to exhibit complexities of character. Characters have patience; but Patience does not have a character. One of the best-known parts of Langland's poem describes the confessions of the Seven Deadly Sins. The personifications are marvellously vivid, but they are not characters. They speak vigorously, but always under the constraint of their signification: Avarice confessing to acts of avarice, Gluttony to gluttony, and so on. Each represents one of the sinful states into which medieval moral theology analysed human behaviour. Like the Freudian scheme of Id, Ego, and Superego, the scheme of the Sins helped people, especially in the confessional, to understand and describe behaviour by resolving it into stable and identifiable constituents. Avarice, sloth, and the rest represent the results of such an analysis.

If, then, personifications are not themselves suitable subjects for analysis, but represent precisely the point at which, in any given text, a writer has chosen to *stop* in the almost endless process of breaking human behaviour down into its constituents, then it follows that the right way to read labelled allegory must be to work up and out from the personifications, so to speak, not down and in to them, as with characters. The interest of personification allegory lies not in the personifications themselves, but in what they do or say; and it is their relationships to each other which will express, in the allegorical fiction, the meaning of the author. Langland's scene between Conscience and Clergy provides a subtle example. The delicate social relationship between a distinguished guest and a host who suddenly 'has to go' served to embody Langland's mixed feelings about the learned Establishment. Gower's *Confessio Amantis* provides another example of the same sort, in the relationship between Venus and her confessor Genius. The delicate relationship here is that between a great lady and the priest who is both a member of her household and also, as confessor, her spiritual father. Genius is both Venus' subordinate and her superior; and Gower uses this social paradox in his attempt to articulate the relation between human love, as represented by Venus, and the mysterious universal forces represented by Genius (a personification derived by Gower from Jean de Meun and the Latin philosophical poets of the twelfth century).

Most Middle English allegories, however, present their persons in relationships simpler than these. The most elementary technique of all is to relate them simply as members of a silent, static group. Such tableaux can form with the greatest ease and naturalness, as in the opening of *Patience*, where an exposition of the eight beatitudes ends like this:

> These arn the happes alle aght that us bihyght weren,
> If we thyse ladyes wolde lof in lyknyng of thewes:
> Dame Povert, dame Pitee, dame Penaunce the thrydde,
> Dame Mekenesse, dame Mercy and miry Clannesse,
> And thenne dame Pes and Pacyence put in theraftter. (29–33)

the happes alle aght] all the eight beatitudes *bihyght*] promised *If . . . thewes*] if we would only honour these ladies by following them in our behaviour

A more artful, and also more frigid, instance of such an allegorical tableau occurs in Chaucer's *Parliament of Fowls* where, outside the temple of Venus, the dreamer sees a group of personifications:

> I saw Beute withouten any atyr,
> And Youthe, ful of game and jolyte;
> Foolhardynesse, Flaterye, and Desyre,
> Messagerye, and Meede, and other thre—
> Here names shul not here be told for me. (225–9)

Messagerye] the sending of (love) messages *Meede*] bribery

This must be one of Chaucer's worst passages. Personifications without names are totally meaningless; and those which are named here are too miscellaneous (unlike the beatitudes) to be merely juxtaposed in this fashion. What is the relation between Youth and Foolhardiness and Flattery? Chaucer was a poet of juxtapositions and unspoken relationships (as between the Tales of the Knight and the Miller). He preferred implication to explication. But personification makes relationships explicit: it is a supremely *articulate* mode. Perhaps this is one reason for Chaucer's general neglect of personification allegory.

Personifications, once they move and speak, can enter into many different kinds of relationship. They can engage in conflict with each other, either with force (battle or siege) or with words (argument or debate).

Conflicts of the first sort commonly take the form of a siege. There is a notable allegorical siege in the *Roman de la Rose*; and Middle English writers are as fond of allegorical sieges as they are of literal ones. The morality play *The Castle of Perseverance* provides a full-scale example. After a wild youth, the hero of this play, Humanum Genus, repents and enters the Castle of Perseverance (also called the Castle of Goodness). The central section is devoted to the siege of the castle by the Seven Deadly Sins, under their three commanders, the World, the Flesh, and the Devil. The Sins, who mount their assaults with banners, slings, and firebrands, are met by the garrison of the Seven Virtues. Langland had used the same allegorical motif for the last episode of *Piers Plowman*. Langland's stronghold (a 'peel' or fortified barn) represents not individual moral strength but the strength of the united Church; and the action is set, not in the everyday time of any man's life, but in historical time. Langland believed that he was living in the last days of the world; and it is Antichrist who leads the final assault upon the barn Unity with which his poem ends. Otherwise the allegory has much in common with that of a morality play: the Sins are personified as 'seven great giants', Sloth uses a sling, and so on.

Armed conflict between virtues and vices is one of the most ancient ways of representing inner moral conflict. A classic text was the *Psychomachia* of the fourth-century poet Prudentius. C. S. Lewis, however, in his influential discussion of the Prudentian tradition in *The Allegory of Love*, points to its limitations: 'While it is true that the *bellum intestinum* [inner battle] is the root of all allegory, it is no less true that only the crudest allegory will represent it by a pitched battle. The abstractions owe their life to the inner conflict; but when once they have come to life, the poet must fetch a compass and dispose his fiction more artfully if he is to succeed' (p. 68). The author of *The Castle of Perseverance* achieves this more artful disposition at the conclusion of his siege. Up to this point, each Sin has approached the walls with a loud, boastful, and threatening speech; and this has been followed by an actual fight. The last of the Sins, however, is Covetousness, and he strikes a quieter and more sinister note:

> How, Mankynde! I am atenyde
> For thou art there so in that holde.
> Cum and speke wyth thi best frende,
> Syr Coveytyse, thou knowyst me of olde.
> What devyl schalt thou ther lenger lende
> Wyth grete penaunce in that castel colde? (2427–32)

atenyde] vexed   *holde*] stronghold   *lenger lende*] stay longer

To this approach Humanum Genus, predisposed to avarice by old age, succumbs without a fight: he deserts the Castle and the Virtues, and resumes his life of sin. The speech of Covetousness creates a strong dramatic effect in performance; and it shows how far personification allegory is, at its best, from weak abstraction. The insidious familiarity of Covetousness does not lack allegorical meaning (the most dangerous faults are those not recognized as alien to our true selves); but it is also most vividly realized, in a tone of plain, man-to-man frankness which anticipates the bluntness of honest Iago.

Langland's siege also ends in imminent defeat; and here too the crisis comes, anticlimactically, in the form of a quiet approach rather than a grand assault. Since wounded men in the garrison need a surgeon, Conscience makes the mistake of admitting into the barn of the Church a certain Friar Flatterer. The Friar offers to cure the wounded men, but instead 'enchants' them with his drugs; and the poem ends with Conscience, as the Sins resume their attack on a now undefended stronghold, setting out to look once more for Piers the Plowman. Thus guile succeeds where force has failed, in *Piers* as in *The Castle*; but Langland characteristically creates an extra challenge for the reader by allowing the literal realities of his age to show through the traditional allegory which represents them. His Friar Flatterer is both, in the siege allegory, a treacherous physician, and also a friar who, like the Friar of Chaucer's Canterbury pilgrimage, betrays men and especially women by granting them easy absolutions.

But however subtly it is handled, the allegory of armed conflict seems to require that one side should be right and the other wrong: it remains an allegory of virtue and vice, black and white. This limitation does not apply, however, to the other kind of conflict in which personifications commonly engage: verbal conflict, or debate. These may themselves involve no more than a simple conflict between right and wrong—the debate between Conscience and Lady Meed in *Piers Plowman* is of this type—but the tradition of debate had its roots in the medieval schools, where students learned rhetorical and logical skills of exposition by arguing cases *in utramque partem*, 'on either side'; and the most interesting literary debates are certainly those which see both sides of a difficult question.

As the scene between Conscience and Clergy shows, Langland can write excellent conversational dialogue for his personifications; but he can also handle the more formal exchanges on a set topic which we call 'debate'. The best example is his debate of the Four Daughters of God in Passus XVIII of the B Text. This is a common bit of personification allegory, with its roots, unusually, in the Bible. Biblical allegory, as we shall see later, does not commonly deal in abstractions; but this passage from the Psalms is an exception: 'Surely his salvation is nigh them that fear him; that glory may dwell in our land. Mercy and truth are met together; righteousness and peace have kissed each other' (85:9–10). Christian writers derived from these verses the idea of a debate about redemption, in which the rival claims of God's justice (represented by Truth and Righteousness) and his mercy (Mercy and Peace) are asserted and finally reconciled, symbolically, in the embrace of the Four Daughters. Most often the scene was set in heaven, either before the Incarnation (as in the 'N town' cycle of mystery plays) or else when man appears for judgement (as at the end of *The Castle of Perseverance*). Langland's imagination, however, was fired by the verse 'Surely his salvation is nigh them that fear him; that glory may dwell in our land'; and he sets the scene, with a wonderful effect of chiaroscuro, in the darkness of Hell, at the moment when, after the Crucifixion, the light or 'glory' of Christ first gleams on the horizon, announcing to 'them that fear him' the Harrowing of Hell. Recalling another Old Testament passage (Isaiah 43:5–6), where God speaks of 'my daughters from the ends of the earth', the poet imagines the daughters coming together each from a different point of the compass: Truth from the east where the sun rises, Mercy from the west where it sets, Righteousness from the 'nyppe of the north', and Peace from the warm south. A scene in which four personifications approach each other in straight lines and right angles sounds unpromising, especially when it is pieced together out of scraps of the Old Testament; but Langland makes it unforgettable, both by his setting—the darkness, the distant light, the tense expectancy—and by the freedom and naturalness with which the personifications behave. These daughters of God are also *sisters*, and they treat each other with sisterly liberty ('Hold thy tongue, Mercy!'). At the same time, the picturesque and dramatic scene retains its primary theological interest. Langland does not, of course, resolve the intractable paradox of a God both just and merciful; but the Daughters do not merely quarrel: they marshal on both sides real and substantial arguments. Here, as in all the best labelled allegory, the analytic mind joins forces with the fictive imagination.

An earlier dream poem in alliterative verse, *Winner and Waster*, probably written in the 1350s and possibly known to Langland, is one of the best Middle English allegorical debates. This brilliant, somewhat neglected poem begins with a vision of two armies, one led by Winner, the other by Waster, drawn up for battle; but the two leaders are summoned by an emissary to the presence of the king, and there, instead of fighting, they argue their respective cases in a debate. The false start is deliberate and significant: substitution of debate for battle marks the poet's intention of presenting, not a conflict between good and evil, but a confrontation between two more or less equal sides in a difficult question. A short passage from Winner's first speech before the king will illustrate both the poet's control of argument *in utramque partem* and the unscholastic richness of his English:

> 'All that I winne thurgh wit, he wastes thurgh pride:
> I gader, I glene, and he lattes go sone;
> I prike and I prine, and he the purse openes.
> Why has this caiteff no care how men corn sellen?
> His londes liggen all ley, his lomes aren solde,
> Down ben his doufehouses, drye ben his pools.
> The devil wonder the wele he weldes at home,
> Bot hunger and hye houses and houndes full kene!'   (230–7)[4]

I prike and I prine] I make everything trim and tidy (?)   *liggen all ley*] all lie untilled   *lomes*] tools   *The devil . . . home*] there is nothing to wonder at in the wealth he commands at home

Winner has a case. His moral charges against Waster (pride here, elsewhere gluttony and lechery) remain unanswered in the poem; and his sketch of an estate made derelict by extravagance and neglect is plausible and disturbing. The estate produces no crops, no fish, and no fowl; and Waster is left with nothing but the gaping vacancies vividly evoked in the last line: human hunger, big empty rooms, and starving dogs. Yet there is also something ridiculous about Winner's indignant and incredulous question: How *can* a man be so unconcerned about corn prices? And the antitheses of the first three lines do not work quite as Winner intends. Opening a purse is not the same thing as wasting through pride; and the tight first-half-lines, with their double alliterations, prepare for the answering charges of avarice and petty meanness which Waster makes in his reply.

Labelled allegory illustrates clearly a general point about allegory: that it has one of its main roots in *language*.[5] Middle English is more of a concrete language than Modern; and wherever, as often happens, a concrete verb is used metaphorically with an abstract noun, there is always the possibility of personification: 'fear held him back' becomes 'Fear held him back'. In Modern English, the act of personification is registered on the page (except at the beginning of sentences and lines of verse) by the substitution of capital letters for lower case; but Middle English scribes did not use capitals as a regular indication of proper names, and the editor frequently meets passages where he is uncertain whether to indicate a personification or not. In such places one can see clearly how personification allegory, far from being a frigid or artificial growth, springs out of the native idiom of Middle English. Sir Gawain, for instance, at the end of his adventure, addresses the Green Knight as follows:

'For care of thy knokke cowardyse me taght
To acorde me with covetyse, my kynde to forsake,
That is larges and lewté that longez to knyghtez.' (2379–81)

Because of my fear of your blow, cowardice taught me to come to terms with
covetousness and so be untrue to my nature, which is that generosity and
fidelity proper to knights

The metaphorical verbs *taght*, *acorde me*, and *forsake* represent the virtues
and vices as persons, like characters in a morality play: Cowardice introduces the hero to Covetousness and encourages him to desert his former
companions, Largess and Lewty. No editor, to my knowledge, has ever
capitalized Cowardice and the rest; but the passage illustrates how spon-
taneously personification can spring out of the metaphors, proverbs, and
idioms of the Middle English language itself. Personification, in such
cases, simply 'makes figures of speech visible', as E. H. Gombrich says of
the political cartoon.[6] Like cartoons, such allegories often display their
linguistic roots. In Langland's story of Lady Meed, for instance, when
Theology intervenes to frustrate the marriage between Meed and False, he
declares that God has promised 'to gyve Mede to Truthe' (B II 120)—an
allegory which derives directly, with word-play on *give*, from one of
Langland's favourite propositions: that God has promised to give the
reward ('mede') of eternal life to those who live a true life ('truthe').

Allegory, however, has another system of roots, through which it draws
not upon language but upon reality. As is well known, the medieval view of
the world was peculiarly favourable to allegory—indeed it is often itself styled
allegorical. Modern minds typically try to understand things and events by
looking for historical or scientific explanations; but medieval men saw
both nature and history as 'books' in which the things and events were to
be understood, not in terms of cause or mechanism, but as a form of
symbolic communication from God to man.[7] St Paul said that 'the invisible
things of him from the creation of the world are clearly seen, being
understood by the things that are made' (Romans 1:20). One twelfth-
century Latin poet expressed this view of the 'things that are made' in
these words:

Omnis mundi creatura
Quasi liber et pictura
Nobis est, et speculum.[8]

The whole created universe is to us like a book, and a picture, and a mirror.

A poet who sees the world as a book in which he can read God's words,
or a picture in which deep truths are represented, or a mirror reflecting his
own condition, will treat birds, animals, trees, flowers, and precious stones

as parts of a common symbolic language. Where he employs this language in allegory, the result is something rather different from personification allegory (though the two types often occur in combination). The difference can be seen by comparing *Winner and Waster* with the earlier debate poem, *The Owl and the Nightingale*. In *Winner and Waster* the opposition between two types of human behaviour is represented in the speeches of disputants who are themselves poetic fictions; but in *The Owl and the Nightingale* a not dissimilar opposition is represented in the speeches of two creatures from the world of nature. Winner and Waster speak with great verve and fluency, but the range of their utterance is determined *a priori* by the abstract opposition which their names declare: the beauty of the poem, as in some of Ben Jonson's plays, lies in rich and energetic detail not spilling over the clear geometrical outlines of the general conception. By contrast, the earlier debate is a somewhat disorderly work. Critics have attempted to stick abstract labels onto the two birds (Gravity and Gaiety, Age and Youth, Philosophy and Art), but without success. The disputants are not personifications. Rather they represent two real species, each with its own characteristic appearance, habitat, and habits. They are both denizens of Nature's realm, and they delight in their own diverse attributes. At one point the Owl says:

> 'Hit is min highte, hit is mi wunne
> That ich me drawe to mine cunde.'   (272–3)

It is my joy and my delight that I live according to my nature.

The author shares this delight; and he fills his poem to overflowing with observation, traditional lore, and stories about owls and nightingales. He writes, indeed, as if no fact about either bird could possibly be irrelevant. Such an assumption may seem irresponsible; but it makes sense once one considers the birds as the product not of evolution but of God. For why *did* God create owls just so, and nightingales just so? It would not be enough to suppose that God was just aiming, in a random way, at variety and plenitude. One would look in every feature and every habit for a meaning, confident that it was there to be found. No part of God's book could be meaningless. It is thinking such as this which supports Nicholas's free and uninhibited development of his bird debate; and the results, though less clear-cut than personification allegory, are more consistent and coherent than a strict Darwinian might expect. The birds, as they defend themselves and attack each other, emerge both as real birds and as allegorical mirrors—*specula*—in which human readers can see their own faces.

It would be possible to give many other examples of the allegory of birds and beasts in Middle English: Chaucer's *Parliament of Fowls*, for example, or Henryson's *Fables*. As Langland observes:

> of briddes and of beestes men by olde tyme
> Ensamples token and termes, as telleth thise poetes.

> (B XII 236–7)

But I shall take my second reading from a different part of the book of nature. Precious stones have always been supposed to possess special powers and meanings; and one of the most elaborately wrought poems of the Ricardian age centres its complex allegory upon a precious stone. *Pearl* concerns the death of a small girl, who appears to the poet in a vision under the name of 'Pearl' (corresponding perhaps to the name Margery in real life). Her clothes are decorated with pearls, she wears a crown 'high pinnacled with clear white pearl', and a single great pearl lies at her breast. As the vision progresses, these pearls prove to express symbolically the whole argument of the poem, for they represent both the spotless innocence of the baptized infant and the eternal reward in heaven which—so the poem argues—is her just reward. The latter meaning is explained by the Pearl maiden herself:

> 'This makellez perle, that boght is dere,
> The joueler gef fore alle hys god,
> Is lyke the reme of hevenesse clere:
> So sayde the Fader of folde and flode;
> For hit is wemlez, clene, and clere,
> And endelez rounde, and blythe of mode,
> And commune to alle that ryghtwys were.'   (733–9)

makellez] matchless   *The joueler . . . god*] for which the jeweller gave all he had   *reme*] realm   *folde*] earth   *wemlez*] spotless   *mode*] spirit

Here, as in the same poet's proof that Gawain's pentangle signifies *trawthe*, the allegorical interpretation stands on the double grounds of authority and the nature of things. The authority in this case is Christ himself, who likened the kingdom of heaven to 'a merchant man, seeking goodly pearls; who, when he had found one pearl of great price, went and sold all that he had, and bought it' (Matthew 13:45–6); but the pearl is also naturally like the kingdom of heaven by virtue of its spherical shape, flawless surface, and luminous whiteness. Colours and shapes, like numbers, formed part of the basic vocabulary—the 'termes', as Langland says—of the book of nature. The sphere is an 'endless' figure, like the more complex pentangle (also called 'endless' in *Gawain* 630); and this endlessness represents, in *Pearl*, the eternal and infinite nature of heavenly joys. The poet's art imitates reality here, for he makes his own creation 'endless round' by linking its last line to its first, so that the poem itself becomes, like its central symbol, an emblem of eternal bliss.

The *Gawain*-poet's reference to Christ's parable of the pearl of great price recalls the fact that medieval poets had, besides the book of nature, another source from which they might draw the terms of their allegories: the book of Scripture. The idea that God communicates with man through these two books is found as late as Sir Thomas Browne, who refers to it in his *Religio Medici* (1643): 'There are two Books from whence I collect my Divinity; besides that written one of God, another of His servant Nature, that universal and publick Manuscript, that lies expans'd unto the Eyes of all: those that never saw him in the one, have discover'd Him in the other'. Parables like that of the pearl of great price are themselves no more than fictional allegories such as a human poet or teacher might invent; but the Bible also was held to exhibit another and more distinctive kind of allegory: the allegory of historical particulars. The events recorded in Scripture belonged to history, not poetic fiction: the record was generally held to be literally true. But history was governed by God's providence; and it was therefore entirely possible that historical particulars might, without prejudice to their historicity, prove to have a further value as figures or types of some higher truth. God is like a poet whose symbols and allegories are *real*. Jerusalem, for instance, is a real city in the Near East; but it is also a God-given type of the (equally real) City of God in heaven. The literal-minded dreamer in *Pearl* objects that the girl cannot be living, as she claims, in Jerusalem, since Jerusalem is a city in Judea (line 922); to which Pearl replies by explaining that there are two Jerusalems, the Old, in which Christ was crucified, and the New, in which he rewards the faithful (937–50).

Medieval interpreters of the Bible customarily distinguish three kinds of higher meaning, which make up, together with the *literal or historical sense*, the so-called 'four levels' of scriptural interpretation. Where the higher meaning refers to the eternal mysteries such as the New Jerusalem, exegetes speak of the *anagogical sense*, distinguishing it from the *moral sense* and (in its narrower signification) the *allegorical sense*. Dante, in his letter to Can Grande about the *Divine Comedy*, illustrates the point by showing how a Biblical reference to the Exodus can be understood in four ways:

> If we inspect the letter alone, the departure of the children of Israel from Egypt in the time of Moses is presented to us; if the allegory, our redemption wrought by Christ; if the moral sense, the conversion of the soul from the grief and misery of sin to the state of grace is presented to us; if the anagogical, the departure of the holy soul from the slavery of this corruption to the liberty of eternal glory.[9]

The 'moral sense' is not a matter of taking events or people from Scripture simply as literal examples of general moral truths, as Cain might be taken as an example of the sin of envy. The use of such examples is very common in medieval literature; it belongs, however, not to the mode of allegory, but to the 'modus exemplificativus', to be discussed later. Allegory, by definition, treats facts or events as metaphors; and moral allegories must be metaphoric, just like any other type. Dante's *Purgatorio* describes the ascent of the poet up the mountain of Purgatory, on whose slopes the various sins are purged, to the Garden of Eden at its top. The Garden of Eden was held to be a real place—like Jerusalem, though even less accessible—but it was also, in Dante and elsewhere, a type of the inno-cence which mankind lost at the Fall. When Dante, at the end of his long and laborious ascent, enters the beautiful garden with its 'foresta spessa e viva' ('dense and living forest'), the moment represents, in one of the richest and most compelling of all medieval allegories, the regaining of Paradise by a descendant of Adam. Purgation and the recovery of inno-cence are possible for any Christian at any time; and it is the special function of moral allegory to represent such individual and everyday experience. This is, as medieval writers put it, the 'quotidian' mode, and its province is the here and now, 'hic et nunc'.

Whereas moral significances belong to everyday time and anagogical ones to eternity, allegorical significances (in the confusing, narrower sense) belong, like the literal events which carry them, to the time of history. In its proper form, allegory (or 'typology', as it is also called) deals in concordances between the Old and New Testaments. Historical par-ticulars from the Old Testament are interpreted as types or figures (*figurae*) of similar particulars in the New, the old history of the Jews being fulfilled by the new history of Christ and his Church. Thus, when Moses strikes the rock in the wilderness and water flows out (Exodus 17:1–6), this is taken as a historical event and as a moral allegory representing the coming of grace to an individual soul in the wilderness of sin; but it also prefigures another moment in history, when a soldier pierced Christ on the cross 'and forthwith came thereout blood and water' (John 19:34). For, as St Paul observed in a seminal passage, 'that Rock was Christ' (1 Corinthians 10:4). Such allegory naturally figures in the mystery cycles, where Old Testa-ment plays form a sequence leading up to the events of Christ's life. The Chester cycle provides an explicit example, in its play of Abraham and Isaac. The story of Abraham's sacrifice of his son could not fail to be taken as a type of God's similar sacrifice; and in the Chester play an Expositor spells out this figural meaning:

'This deede yee seene done here in this place,
In example of Jesus done yt was,
That for to wynne mankinde grace
Was sacrifyced one the roode.

By Abraham I may understand
The Father of heaven that cann fonde
With his Sonnes blood to breake that bonde
That the dyvell had brought us to.'   (464–71)

cann fonde] set out

This figural way of looking at events is not confined to the history recorded in the Bible. God's providential order is most clearly apparent in the history of Jews and Christians recorded there; but the same order can be found expressed in similar connections elsewhere. The Tale told by the Prioress in Chaucer's *Canterbury Tales*, for instance, concerns an event in recent, or at least post-scriptural, times: the murder of a Christian school-boy by Jews. Modern readers naturally understand this story in terms of the modern Jewish question; but several passages in the Tale suggest a different way of looking at it. When the Prioress addresses the Jewish murderers as 'cursed folk of Herodes al newe' (VII 574), the apostrophe is not merely abusive: it suggests that the Jews are here re-enacting ('al newe') the massacre of the innocents by Herod, recorded in the Gospels. Just as Old Testament events prefigure the New, so here a New Testament event is, as it were, 'postfigured' in modern times. This interpretation is confirmed later, when the Prioress refers to the grieving mother of the murdered innocent as 'this newe Rachel' (627). 'A voice was heard in Ramah, lamentation, and bitter weeping; Rachel weeping for her children, refused to be comforted for her children, because they were not': this passage from the prophecies of Jeremiah (31:15) was cited by St Matthew in his account of Herod's massacre of the innocents: 'Then was fulfilled that which was spoken by Jeremy the prophet, saying . . .' (Matthew 2:17). Like the mothers of the innocents, the mother of the murdered boy is a 'new Rachel': modern history looks back to the same cardinal events to which Old Testament history and prophecy look forward. Modern experience re-enacts those events, both in historical reality and in the symbolism of the liturgical year. The Prioress, as scholars have noted, draws freely on the Mass for Holy Innocents' Day in telling her tale of a latter-day innocent.

This chapter has spoken of allegorical writing as having two main systems of roots: one embedded in the language itself, the other in the realities of nature and history. Some works draw more heavily on the one, some on the other; and to that extent it is possible to speak of 'labelled allegories', or to distinguish, as another critic does, between 'personification allegories' and 'symbol allegories'. But such distinctions are far from absolute; and many of the best writings of this period draw freely on both kinds of root, combining personifications and other labelled allegories with allegories derived from the two books of Nature and Scripture. Langland was particularly skilled at such combinations; and this discussion of allegory will conclude with an extended example which shows the mode at its freest and most challenging.

Langland's account of the Passion of Christ, represented as a joust between the Christ-knight and the powers of evil, is justly famous; but the build-up to that climactic episode illustrates equally well the poet's powerful way with allegory. Just as in Passus XVIII he introduces the Four Daughters of God into the Harrowing of Hell, so here, in Passus XVI-XVII, he blends scriptural history with personification, drawing also upon one of Christ's parables. From each of these three realms—history and personification and parable—Langland derives a triad, and these reveal, when they are superimposed one upon the other, rich doctrinal and structural harmonies. The three triads are as follows: Faith, Hope, and Charity, personified; Abraham, Moses, and Christ, from scriptural history; and the Priest, the Levite, and the Samaritan, from the parable of the Good Samaritan.

Such a triad of triads might appear to be, at best, like the five fives of the pentangle in *Sir Gawain*, an ingenious piece of number symbolism. In the event, however, Langland derives from it an allegorical action both complex in its doctrinal implications and also, as a story, energetic and inventive. The action begins with Will waking from his dream-within-a-dream of the tree of Charity and finding himself in a dream world newly charged with expectancy by the prospect of Christ's joust with the Devil, which is now imminent. The atmosphere, in fact, is that of Cup Final day, with men streaming towards Jerusalem; but Will does not know what is going on, and his first encounter only increases his bewilderment:

> And thanne mette I with a man, a myd-Lenten Sonday,
> As hoor as an hawethorn, and Abraham he highte.
> I frayned hym first fram whennes he come,
> And of whennes he were, and whider that he thoughte.
> 'I am Feith,' quod that freke, 'it falleth noght me to lye,
> And of Abrahames hous an heraud of armes.
> I seke after a segge that I seigh ones,
> A ful bold bacheler—I knew hym by his blasen.' (XVI 172–9)

hoor] white *highte*] was called *frayned*] asked *freke*] man *segge*] man
bacheler] young knight *blasen*] blazon, heraldic arms

Mention of Mid-Lent Sunday, the fourth Sunday in Lent, places the action at a point in the liturgical year corresponding to the moment in history which Langland has in mind, when redemption was imminent. Also, the Epistle read on this Sunday was Galatians 4:22–31, in which Paul speaks of Abraham and interprets his two sons, Isaac and Ishmael, as types of the old and new covenants. The original readers would therefore have been half-prepared for the meeting which follows. The old man, vividly 'white as a hawthorn bush', is Abraham (who lived to be 175), but like Paul's Abraham he is also something else. The phrase 'and Abraham he highte' suggests that Will does not identify him as *the* Abraham; and the ancient, when he speaks, identifies himself as Faith. Abraham was a familiar scriptural type of faith (as in Romans 4); but a character who calls himself Faith cannot be quite the historical Abraham, even though he says he belongs to 'Abraham's house'. The speaker's identity is further complicated when he claims to be a herald of arms. One of the functions of heralds was to identify knights at jousts by their coats of arms and announce them to the watching crowds. Faith's claim to be a herald therefore associates him with the forthcoming joust; and it is also allegorically appropriate, since faith identifies and declares the hidden godhead of Christ. At the same time, when Faith speaks of seeking a bold knight whom he has already seen, he speaks also in the person of Abraham, as his subsequent words make clear. After expounding the doctrine of the Trinity, he declares:

> 'Thus in a somer I hym seigh as I sat in my porche.
> I roos up and reverenced hym, and right faire hym grette.
> Thre men, to my sighte, I made wel at ese,
> Wessh hir feet and wiped hem, and afterward thei eten
> Calves flessh and cakebreed, and knewe what I thoughte.'
>
> (XVI 225–9)

These beautiful lines are entirely derived, apart from the wiping of the feet, from the account in Genesis 18 of the mysterious visitation of 'three men' to Abraham before the destruction of Sodom and Gomorrah. Following tradition, Langland takes the three men as types of the Trinity: a prefiguration of New Testament truth granted to an Old Testament man of faith. But he also, characteristically, preserves the historical and physical reality of the event (the heat, the calves' flesh, and the cakebread), just as the *Gawain*-poet does in his fuller rendering of the same episode in *Cleanness* (601ff.).

After Abraham/Faith has finished speaking, the pace quickens:

> I wepte for hise wordes. With that saugh I another
> Rapeliche renne forth the righte wey he wente.
> I affrayned hym first fram whennes he come,
> What he highte and whider he wolde—and wightly he tolde.

'I am *Spes*, a spie,' quod he, 'and spire after a knyght
That took me a maundement upon the mount of Synay
To rule alle reames therewith—I bere the writ here.'

(XVI 272–XVII 3)

Rapeliche renne] swiftly run   *affrayned*] asked   *highte*] was called   *wightly*] promptly   *spire*] ask   *maundement*] commandment

The declaration 'I am *Spes*' matches 'I am Feith' in XVI 176; but this figure is not simply a personification either. When he speaks of receiving the commandment on Mount Sinai, he identifies himself with Moses; and although he is never called Moses, his subsequent talk with Will confirms that we are here concerned with the Mosaic law. This is the first written law, inscribed on the 'piece of hard rock' which Spes carries with him (XVII 10). It superseded the unwritten law of nature which, according to medieval belief, governed all men (including Abraham) before the time of Moses; but it is in its turn to be superseded by a third law, that of Christ. Hence Moses, a man who lived in hope of the Promised Land and sent spies to view it (Numbers 13), is represented as himself a spy, searching for the knight who will set the seal upon the law which he carries, completing it with the sign of the cross (XVII 6). The expectation of Christ, who will bring his new law of Charity, the supreme theological virtue surpassing Faith and Hope, has now reached the point when it is to be satisfied. But it is satisfied in a brilliantly unexpected fashion. Will, Faith/Abraham, and Spes/Moses make their way towards Jerusalem, talking together:

Thanne seighe we a Samaritan sittynge on a mule,
Ridynge ful rapely the righte wey we yeden,
Comynge from a contree that men called Jerico—
To a justes in Jerusalem he jaced awey faste.   (XVII 50–3)

rapely] swiftly   *yeden*] went   *jaced*] galloped

The Samaritan of Christ's parable was generally thought of as travelling, like the wounded man, 'down from Jerusalem to Jericho' (Luke 10:30); but Langland's Samaritan is hurrying towards Jerusalem, like Will and his companions. Indeed, in a powerfully dream-like way, he is implicitly identified with the jouster Christ himself; for it is not the Samaritan but Christ who rides—and enters Jerusalem—on the back of a mule. This identification is left implicit, like that of the Samaritan with Charity; but both are firmly suggested when Langland has Faith/Abraham and Spes/Moses play the parts of the Priest and the Levite in the parable, both of whom passed by on the other side when they saw the wounded man:

Feith hadde first sighte of hym, ac he fleigh aside,
And nolde noght neghen hym by nyne londes lengthe.
Hope cam hippynge after, that hadde so ybosted
How he with Moyses maundement hadde many men yholpe;
Ac whan he hadde sighte of that segge, aside he gan hym drawe
Dredfully, bi this day, as doke dooth fram the faucon!

(XVII 59–64)

ac] but   *fleigh*] flinched   *neghen*] approach   *londes*] ridges of ploughland
hippynge] hopping   *yholpe*] helped   *segge*] man   *doke*] duck

The comedy of this sharp little scene marks the limitations of Faith and Hope, Abraham and Moses, the Natural and the Mosaic laws: none of them could save fallen man, who had to wait for the coming of Christ the Samaritan to bind up his wounds and take him to be cared for at an inn.

In the parable, the Samaritan leaves the wounded man at the inn; and Langland's Samaritan also departs, to continue his journey to Jerusalem, pursued with pathetic eagerness by Will, Faith, and Spes. Will catches up and receives his instruction; but the dream ends with the eager Samaritan spurring his mount and galloping away to Jerusalem:

'I may no lenger lette!' quod he, and lyard he prikede,
And wente awey as wynd—and therwith I awakede.

(XVII 352–3)

lette] delay   *lyard*] his horse

The stage is set for Langland's vision of Christ's entry into Jerusalem, at the beginning of the next dream:

Oon semblable to the Samaritan, and somdeel to Piers the Plowman,
Barefoot on an asse bak bootles cam prikye.

(XVIII 10–11)

One like the Samaritan and somewhat like Piers the Plowman came spurring barefoot without boots on an ass's back.

This association of the already composite figure of Samaritan/Christ/Charity with Piers the Plowman, himself a figure of great complexity, raises issues which cannot be discussed here. Passus XVI and XVII are sufficient to illustrate Langland's mastery of such complex associations, linking history, personification, and parable into an allegorical action which drives forward towards its climax. The invention of an allegory such as this requires an athletic strength and agility in the poet's mind and imagination; and it requires of the reader a corresponding athletic response.

II

In the last of Robert Henryson's collection of Aesopic fables, the Scots poet tells, with his customary skill, the story of the Toad and the Mouse: how a mouse, wanting to cross a river, accepts the help of a deceitful toad; how the toad, in the middle of the river, tries to drown the mouse; and how both mouse and toad are snatched up and eaten by a kite. There follows the traditional exposition or Moralitas, divided here into two parts. The second part (2934–68) interprets the fable allegorically: the mouse betokens the soul, bound to the body as the mouse binds herself to the ugly toad; the turbulent river is the world, with its 'waves of tribulation'; and the kite is death, which carries man suddenly off. This is a neat example of that allegorical way of understanding stories which governed so much medieval reading, not only of the Bible, but also of Classical authors such as Ovid and Virgil. But Henryson precedes this allegorization with three stanzas, marked off by a refrain and contrasting stanza-form, which moralize the story in a different and simpler fashion:

> My brother, gif thow will tak advertence,
> Be this fabill thow may persave and se
> It passis far all kynd of pestilence
> Ane wickit mynd with wordis fair and sle.
> Be war thairfore with quhome thow fallowis the,
> For thow wer better beir of stane the barrow,
> Or sweitand dig and delf quhill thow may dre,
> Than to be matchit with ane wickit marrow.　　　　　(2910–7)

> *advertence*] warning　*fallowis the*] associate yourself　*thow ... barrow*] it would be better for you to carry a hand-barrow full of stones　*sweitand*] sweating　*delf*] dig　*dre*] last　*matchit*] matched　*marrow*] companion

This warning against the 'fair and sly' words of wicked companions is derived from the story without any allegorical translation (beyond that required by all animal fables): the story literally illustrates, or exemplifies, the point. Henryson himself apparently alludes to this distinction between the two parts of his Moralitas when, at its end, he ironically instructs the reader how to reply if anyone asks him why the poem stops so abruptly:

> Say thow, I left the laif unto the freiris,
> To mak a sample or similitude.　　　　　(2971–2)

> *laif*] rest

'Samples' (*exempla*) and allegorical 'similitudes' provided medieval teachers and preachers—not least the friars, to whom Henryson alludes—with their two main ways of illustrating and enforcing an argument. Thus, one fourteenth-century treatise on composing sermons advises the preacher to 'expound some sweet allegory [*aliquam dulcem allegoriam*] and narrate some delightful example [*aliquid jocundum exemplum*], so that the profundity of the allegory may delight the learned and the simplicity [*levitas*] of the example edify the ignorant'.[10] Chaucer's Pardoner, as we saw, also regarded *exempla* as suitable for 'lewed peple'. Exemplification is certainly a less complex mode than allegory; and it is perhaps this relative simplicity or *levitas* which has led modern critics to devote little attention to it. Although prejudice against allegory is not dead, the arguments of such different advocates as C. S. Lewis, Rosemond Tuve, and D. W. Robertson have restored respectability to the mode. By comparison, little attention has been paid to 'exemplification'—as the unfamiliarity of the term itself shows. The process by which general truths are derived from particular instances, fictional or not, may seem too universal and familiar to require special discussion. Also, the distinguishing features of *exemplum* run counter to the inclination to look in literature for precisely those truths which *cannot* be stated as generalizations. Explicit statement of general truth and formal subordination of particular instance are features which do not commend themselves to most modern readers. Also, it may be suggested that exemplification, unlike allegory, assumed a view of the past which, for the last two hundred years or so, has been unpopular. History, in the old tag, was *magistra vitae*—a mistress who taught you how to live, by providing examples of what to do and what not to do. Medieval treatises on statecraft, for instance, differ from their modern counterparts in demonstrating their general propositions with examples drawn from the past, and especially from the history of Greece and Rome. When Thomas Hoccleve, in his *Regement of Princes*, wishes to show that lords should be faithful to their pledged word, he does so by telling the story of Marcus Regulus, the classic example of such fidelity (*Regement* 2248–96). He would have agreed with Montaigne, who says that men should be 'spectators or observers of other mens lives and actions, that so they may the better judge and direct their owne. Unto examples may all the most profitable Discourses of Philosophie be sorted, which ought to be the touch-stone of humane actions, and a rule to square them by' (Book I Chapter XXV, Florio's translation).

Exemplary figures and stories are found everywhere in medieval art and literature, especially from the twelfth century on. Dante, using the language of scholastic literary theory in his letter to Can Grande, says that the mode (*modus*) of the *Divine Comedy* is exemplary (*exemplorum positivus*). In the *Purgatorio*, for instance, each of the seven deadly sins is represented in its own circle by a set of *exempla*, matched in each case by another set representing the corresponding virtue. Thus in the circle of the proud, images engraved in the marble side of the mountain confront the penitents with types of humility: the Virgin Mary at the Annunciation, King David dancing before the ark of God, and the Roman Emperor Trajan submitting to the demands of a poor widow (*Purgatorio* X 28–99). These 'images of humility' illustrate several of the characteristic features of exemplary narrative. It is, for one thing, appropriate that they should appear in bas-relief, contrasting with the fully three-dimensional beings who pass and see them. Exemplary narrative tends to flatten its characters, in so far as it sees them only from the point of view of the general truth in question—the humble King of the Jews, the humble Queen of Heaven, the humble Emperor of Rome. The same concern for *general* truth leads also to a loss of historical perspective, and hence another kind of flattening, symbolized in the *Purgatorio* by the fact that David, Mary, and Trajan all appear without distinction on the same rock surface. Later in the same circle (XII 16–72) Dante and Virgil come upon examples of pride carved into the surface of the pavement underfoot, again without distinction: exemplary figures from Old Testament history (Nimrod), ancient history (Cyrus), and classical myth (Arachne). Distinctions between Christian and pagan, myth and history, are neutralized in such collections of *exempla*, whose concern is to provide, from whatever source, a 'touch-stone of humane actions'. Gower's *Confessio Amantis* flattens out its stories in the same way, for purposes of moral instruction. When Genius is helping the penitent Amans to confess his sins of pride, for instance, he illustrates the different branches of the sin with a range of stories matching Dante's: a fairy-tale (Florent), classical myths (Narcissus, Capaneus), an episode from the Old Testament (Nebuchadnezzar), another from ancient history (Mundus and Paulina), and so on. The secular character of the *Confessio* excludes examples from the New Testament; but otherwise Gower's poem exhibits the typical eclecticism of the exemplary mode.

Exemplary figures and stories may be invoked to demonstrate a wide variety of different kinds of general truth. In the *Canterbury Tales* Dorigen uses them to prove that death is better than dishonour, Chantecleer to prove that dreams reveal the future. But Dante's use of *exempla* to illustrate sins and virtues represents a kind of exemplary writing particularly important from the thirteenth to the fifteenth century. The scheme of the seven deadly sins itself goes back to St Gregory the Great (sixth century); but in the twelfth and thirteenth centuries, scholastic philosophers took it over as part of a new and elaborately analytic moral psychology.[11] This scholastic theorizing about virtues and vices was at first confined to the schools; but after the Fourth Lateran Council (1215–16), when the Church required every member to go to confession at least once a year, moral psychology became a matter of more general interest. To confess his sins, a penitent had to be able to identify and name them. Accordingly, the Church produced a mass of handbooks, treatises, and encyclopaedias for priests, in which virtues and vices were systematically expounded in all their ramifications, for purposes of the confessional. Perhaps the most important of these handbooks was the *Summa de Vitiis et Virtutibus* of William Perrault, or Peraldus (mid-thirteenth century). Recent scholarship has shown that both Dante (in *Purgatorio* XVII) and Chaucer (in the *Parson's Tale*) depended for their treatment of the sins upon this work, so obscure to us.[12] Confessional moral psychology had, in fact, profound consequences for the literature of the later Middle Ages. It encouraged the kind of searching self-awareness displayed by Sir Gawain in his confession to the Green Knight, quoted earlier; and it made writers much more conscious of, and articulate about, the moral issues raised by their stories. Such definition of moral issues will be particularly sharp, of course, where the story is told as an *exemplum* of some named virtue or vice, as in the *Purgatorio*, or *Confessio Amantis*, or Chaucer's *Pardoner's Tale*, or the *Gawain*-poet's *Patience*.

Left to themselves, most stories will raise a multitude of issues. To present them as *exempla*, therefore, an author or speaker must impose an intention upon them: the story demonstrates *this*, or *that*. The rhetorician Matthew of Vendôme states the rule of interpretation which follows from this: 'Examples must be referred back to the intention of the exemplifier' [*exempla ad mentem exemplificantis debent retorqueri*].[13] The 'intention of the exemplifier' should appear in the selective highlighting of those features of the story which are most relevant to the general truth he has in mind. An *exemplum* is itself, etymologically considered, something taken out as a sample (from Latin *eximere* to take out); but a further selection of the relevant features within an *exemplum* usually proves necessary. One author of a collection of *exempla* for preachers states this necessity baldly: 'If it is a long story, useless or less useful things must be cut out, and only what is relevant to the subject must be narrated' [*solum quod facit ad rem est narrandum*].[14] Dante's examples of humility show how, in the hands of a master, this highly selective method can produce stylish results:

> The angel who came to earth proclaiming
> The peace which had been mourned for many years,
> So opening heaven, long under interdict,
>
> Appeared before us, so faithfully
> Sculpted there, in a gentle attitude,
> That he did not appear a dumb image.

You would have sworn that he was saying 'Ave!'
For there also was the image of her
Who turned the keys to open the exalted love;

And her attitude was marked with those words:
Ecce ancilla Dei, as distinctly
As any figure stamped upon wax.

(*Purgatorio* X 34–45)

Dante himself treats the story of the Annunciation here like warm wax, stamping upon it his intended meaning, which is to present both Gabriel and Mary as types of humility.

Readers of English poetry most often have their first encounter with this kind of writing in Chaucer's *Canterbury Tales*, in the story which the Pardoner tells as an *exemplum* of avarice. Here and elsewhere, Chaucer displays a marked scepticism about the exemplary mode, or at least about its workings in practice. The murderous climax of the Pardoner's story illustrates his theme forcefully and directly, as a good *exemplum* should, showing how avarice is indeed the root or *radix* from which other evils grow; but if, following Matthew of Vendôme, the reader refers back to the *mens exemplificantis* or 'intention of the exemplifier', he encounters a blatant contradiction between that intention and the moral theme. When the Pardoner declares 'I preche of no thyng but for coveityse' (VI 424), the shift of preposition from *of* to *for* indicates that covetousness is his motive as well as his theme. He is a 'vicious man' telling a 'moral tale'. He is not only an *exemplificans* but also himself an *exemplum* of exactly the vice against which he preaches, so that his final discomfiture at the hands of the Host may be seen as a mild, real-life equivalent to the lurid fate suffered by the young men in his story.

There are many other instances in the *Canterbury Tales* of such discrepancy between *exemplum* and *mens exemplificantis*. It is one of Chaucer's favourite comic themes: a character will employ impeccable examples to prove some point of prudence or ethics which he quite ignores in his own life. History may be *magistra vitae*; but she is, in Chaucer, an ineffective mistress. The worldly and 'well-faring' Monk narrates a series of 'ensamples trewe and olde' (VII 1998) to prove the fickleness of fortune and the vanity of the world. Chantecleer, in the story told by the Nun's Priest, makes a long speech to his wife in which he proves that dreams do have prophetic meaning, employing in the process two vivid and sinister *exempla* about nameless characters (VII 2984–3104), backed up with named examples from modern times (St Kenelm), antiquity (Scipio, Croesus, Andromache), and the Old Testament (David, Joseph); yet at the end of it all, one glance at his attractive wife is enough to dispel his apprehensions; and when dawn comes, he defies his dream and goes out into the farmyard. In the *Summoner's Tale*, again, the Friar makes a long speech to the peasant Thomas against the sin of wrath (III 2005–93), proving his point, as a friar would, with examples of an unnamed 'irous potestat', of 'irous Cambises', and of 'irous Cirus'; but the immediate effect of his sermon is only to make Thomas 'ny wood for ire'. Indeed, he responds to the Friar's hypocrisy with an insult so crude that the Friar himself falls into a furious rage, quite unable to control the passion against which he could preach so eloquently: 'He grynte with his teeth, so was he wrooth'.

In these instances, comedy respects the time-honoured claim of exemplary stories to demonstrate general truths. There is nothing wrong with Chantecleer's stories: they do indeed demonstrate an important truth, as subsequent events in the farmyard prove. If the exemplary mode breaks down here, or in the tales of the Pardoner and Summoner, it is simply because people are too weak or too wicked to heed the voice of history and traditional wisdom. Elsewhere, however, we find some medieval writers dealing with more problematic cases, where the fundamental exemplary relation between story and general truth is itself in question. Modern readers, who in any case tend to regard a straight moral as intrinsically naïve and even sub-literary, are particularly drawn to such problematic cases. In Middle English they occur chiefly in the more sophisticated writings of the fourteenth and fifteenth centuries: in Gower's *Confessio Amantis*, for instance.

Gower's narrative art has been widely praised; but concentration on his stories, both in critical discussions and in volumes of selections, has tended to draw attention away from the context in which the stories are embedded: the Lover's confession to Genius. All the stories are told by the priest Genius, as he leads Amans in his confession through the seven deadly sins. As in earlier confessional works, such as Robert Mannyng's *Handlyng Synne*, the stories provide illustrations of sins to be confessed and models of virtues to be emulated. Thus at one point Amans asks for 'som good ensample' to show him how to avoid foolish haste, and Genius replies:

> 'Mi sone, that thou miht enforme
> Thi pacience upon the forme
> Of olde essamples, as thei felle,
> Now understond what I schal telle.'
>
> (III 1753–6)

'Olde essamples' (in this case a story from the aftermath of the Trojan siege) provide a model or 'forme' upon which present conduct can be 'informed'. This is the classic doctrine of *historia magistra vitae*, upon which the exemplary mode depends. However, Gower's stories do not always function so straightforwardly. Sometimes it seems that he has simply failed to find a suitable story to illustrate this vice or that virtue, as required by his scheme; but on other occasions we can recognize a deliberate finesse in the relation between tale and context. Most often these finesses derive, as in the similar case of Chaucer's *Legend of Good Women*, from something equivocal in the 'intention of the exemplifier'. Genius normally speaks as a loyal follower of Venus, arguing in the cause of Love (*in amoris causa*, as Gower's Latin sidenotes have it) against those 'vices' which hinder courtly passion. But he is also a priest, to whom Venus herself must submit in confession; and as a priest he can and does take a larger view, not necessarily coinciding with Venus'. This larger view can create complications in the interpretation even of those *exempla* which Genius explicitly refers to Love's cause. Thus at the beginning of Book IV, which is devoted to the sin of sloth, a Latin sidenote announces 'an *exemplum* against those who sin by delaying in matters of love' [*exemplum contra istos qui in amoris causa tardantes delinquunt*, opposite IV 80]. This turns out to be the story of how Aeneas, by failing to return to Carthage, caused the death of Dido. The story is told from Dido's point of view, as in Ovid's *Heroides*, with only a passing reference to the Virgilian theme of Aeneas' high destiny in Italy (IV 92–3); yet even so it seems a strange example of delay or procrastination in love. Genius loyally makes the best of the case, saying that Aeneas,

> which hadde hise thoghtes feinte
> Towardes love and full of slowthe,
> His time lette, and that was rowthe.   (118–20)

feinte] sluggish   *lette*] missed   *rowthe*] a pity

But Aeneas had apparently had no intention of returning, and had promised no 'time'. In any case, the story hardly amounts to a recommendation of busyness (as against sloth) in matters of love, for it was that which led Dido to her tragic suicide. The story ends with a distinctly enigmatic summary:

> And thus sche gat hireselve reste
> In remembrance of alle slowe.   (136–7)

slowe] slothful ones

But is not 'sloth in love' itself an easier road to that 'reste' which Dido so painfully achieves? The poem resolves this enigma only in its closing pages, where Amans finally abandons 'Love's cause'.

Gower's tale is short (61 lines) and sketchy. When the scale of the narrative is increased, complications of a different sort may arise; for those details of human motive and behaviour which show up in larger-scale narrative tend to put at risk the general truth which the story claims to exemplify. In literature as in life, events often appear less simple the more you know about them. Most stories, if they are told with any richness of human detail, tend to forfeit their straightforward relationship to exemplified truth. In the light of such a story, the 'truth' may come to seem complicated, or doubtful, or simply irrelevant. Large-scale exemplary stories of this sort are a characteristic product of later medieval literature, in England and elsewhere. In Boccaccio's *Decameron*, for instance, most of the stories are told to illustrate some theme or topic prescribed by a member of the company (e.g. 'the fortunes of such as after divers misadventures have at last attained a goal of unexpected felicity'); but the stories outgrow this purpose. In many, the formal exemplary intention is little more than a scrap of eggshell sticking to the chicken's side. But this development is not simply a matter of breaking out of the constraints of the exemplary mode. Stories of this sort at their best combine wealth of fictional detail with a control of thematic significance derived from the discipline of *exemplum*. This combination, where it is found, in Boccaccio or Chaucer, represents an important stage in the development of narrative art in Europe. No doubt all stories have meaning; but ways of articulating meaning evolve gradually, and in this evolution the *exemplum* played its part. Medieval preachers developed a set of five-finger exercises, one might say, which made possible the more sophisticated skills of Chaucer, Boccaccio, and their successors.

Chaucer's *Clerk's Tale* (derived, via Petrarch's Latin version, from the *Decameron*) illustrates such large-scale exemplary fiction at its most difficult. Stories which are adopted as *exempla* tend to be of an extreme kind, illustrating some virtue or vice with a conspicuous and out-of-the-ordinary instance. Regulus does not simply keep his word: he keeps it with an enemy, knowing that he will lose his life in consequence. The Clerk's story of Griselda is even more extreme. The heroine, suffering a series of terrible wrongs inflicted on her by her husband, exemplifies wifely patience in the highest possible degree. Narrated on a small scale, in the bare and abstract manner of the *exemplum*-books, the story might pass muster as an 'old essample', an ideal model upon which some keen young wife might actually attempt to 'inform her patience'. But when it is fleshed out, as by Boccaccio and his imitators, the stable relationship between story and moral is violently disturbed. How could Walter behave as he does? And how could Griselda bear it? Should she, indeed, have borne it? Dioneo, who tells the story in the *Decameron*, begins by explaining that it does not, like the other stories of the day, present an example of 'magnificent' behaviour, but rather a 'piece of mad folly' on Walter's part 'which I counsel none to copy'; and at the end of the story, the ladies' response is doubtful, 'one inclining to censure where another found matter for commendation'.[15] Petrarch made his Latin version under the heading 'Concerning the Notable Obedience and Fidelity of a Wife'; but both he and Chaucer's Clerk following him disclaim at the end any intention of presenting Griselda as a model to be followed by modern wives:

> This storie is seyd, nat for that wyves sholde
> Folwen Grisilde as in humylitee,
> For it were inportable, though they wolde;
> But for that every wight, in his degree,
> Sholde be constant in adversitee
> As was Grisilde; therfore Petrak writeth
> This storie, which with heigh stile he enditeth.
>
> For, sith a womman was so pacient
> Unto a mortal man, wel moore us oghte
> Receyven al in gree that God us sent;
> For greet skile is, he preeve that he wroghte. (IV 1142–52)

inportable] unbearable   *enditeth*] composes   *in gree*] with good will *For . . . wroghte*] for it is very reasonable that he should test what he has made

The disclaimer, borrowed from Petrarch, is given a humorous Chaucerian twist by the ambiguous word 'inportable', meaning either (as Petrarch says) that modern wives could not bear what Griselda did, or else that it would be unbearable for the rest of us if they *could*. Either way, the comment registers once again Chaucer's ironic sense of the gap between *exempla* and actual human behaviour. The *a fortiori* application which follows ('wel moore us oghte. .') shifts the mode from example to similitude, proposing what is in effect an allegorical reading of the story by taking Walter as a type of God 'proving what he has made'. After this, however, the Clerk reverts to literal interpretation, when he again advises wives not to imitate the patience of Griselda. The final effect is very equivocal. We hardly know in the end what to make of the story—except that it is plainly *not* a simple example of 'the notable obedience and fidelity of a wife'.

The ironies and complexities of the exemplary mode in Chaucer and Gower present problems with which modern readers are, on the whole, well equipped to deal. So much so, indeed, that it seems necessary to affirm that exemplification can achieve good results which are not ironic or problematical. Simple and straightforward *exempla* may, of course, be simply and straightforwardly dull; but they can also, in the right hands, be rich and satisfying. A case in point is the Ricardian poem commonly known as *Patience*. As its (modern) title suggests, the moral theme of this poem resembles that of the *Clerk's Tale*; but in this case there can be no serious doubts about the intention of the exemplifier, or about the relationship between the story and its moral. The poem announces its theme boldly and plainly in the opening line ('Pacience is a poynt, thagh hit displese ofte'), identifies it as one of eight virtues to which rewards are promised in the beatitudes, and proceeds to the *exemplum* of Jonah, which occupies almost all the rest of the work. The story of Jonah, narrated with much lively detail, touches the moral theme at several points. Jonah himself is an example of impatience, for he fails on three occasions to 'receyven al in gree that God him sent': first in his refusal to undertake God's mission to Nineveh, then his rebellious anger (410–11) at God's decision to spare the penitent city, and finally his comic indignation (481) when God destroys his sheltering woodbine. By contrast, God sets an example of patience and 'soffraunce' (417) in his treatment both of Jonah and of the Ninevites. This multiple relation, positive and negative, between story and moral does not, however, bring with it any of the doubts and ironies which disturb the simple functioning of the exemplary mode in the *Clerk's Tale*.

Modern criticism has on the whole found this straightforward exemplary character of *Patience* something of an embarrassment. One response, which accommodates the poem to our idea of literary discourse, has been to wrap it in a saving membrane of fiction, by emphasizing the dramatic and fictive status of the 'preaching' narrator. Failing that, criticism has concentrated on those features of the narrative itself which distinguish it from the run-of-the-mill small-scale sermon *exemplum*—the marvellously circumstantial description of Jonah in the whale's belly, for instance. But the undoubted vividness of the story should not divert attention from its exemplary point. On the contrary, it is because the story is so vivid that it makes its point so forcibly; and if we fail to see this, it can only be from a profound failure of interest in general moral concepts. We do not *want* to learn about patience. Current literary thinking, reflecting a general tendency in ethical thought, stresses the unique complexity of the individual case, and regards with suspicion abstract moral categories such as the old Virtues and Vices, especially when these are arranged in schemes. But the point of these categories may be misunderstood. No one of any sense ever supposed that each human action, let alone each human being, could be adequately described in terms of a single moral idea. Rather, the application of those ideas to particular cases was a delicate and difficult art, cultivated under the name of 'casuistry'. It is casuistry (though the term is, significantly, now always abusive) when the hero of

Sir Gawain analyses his single fault into three moral constituents, cowardice, covetousness, and untruth (2379–84). Yet such subtle analyses are hardly possible without commonly understood categories and terms; and these categories—in the Middle Ages, the virtues and vices—cannot simply be taken for granted, for they tend to become weakened and coarsened with the passage of time. To reinforce and refine the categories themselves is therefore a perennial need in any society, Christian or otherwise. The Middle Ages met this need both by theoretical exposition (treatises on vices and virtues) and by *exempla*. It is not the business of such *exempla* to offer marginal or problematic 'cases' for lawyers, or casuists, or literary critics to get their teeth into. The proper position of such stories is at the centre, not at the margins, of the moral idea which they exemplify; and any richness or complexity in the story should ideally serve to display some corresponding richness or complexity at the centre of the master-idea itself.

The story of Jonah functions like that in *Patience*. The poem directs attention through its *exemplum* towards the central core of a moral idea which was (potentially, at least) much richer then than it is now. In his introductory passage on the beatitudes, the poet associates patience with the eighth: 'blessed are they which are persecuted for righteousness' sake'. The poet would have known this verse (Matthew 5:10) in its Vulgate Latin form: 'beati, qui persecutionem *patiuntur* propter justitiam'. His very free rendering of this makes the main point straight away: 'Thay ar happen also that con her hert stere' ('blessed are they also who can *govern their hearts*', 27). Patience is the virtue which establishes man's control over the feelings, emotions, and passions of his heart. Christ said: 'In your patience possess ye your hearts' (Luke 21:19); and speaking of this possession or control, St Thomas Aquinas wrote: 'Man is said to possess his soul by patience, in so far as it removes by the root the passions that are evoked by hardship and disturb the soul' (*Summa Theologica* 2–2 q.136 a.2). Patience is chiefly concerned with the 'passions that are evoked by hardship' [*passiones adversitatum*], rather than by what the scholastics call the 'concupiscible' passions aroused by objects of desire. That is why Patience, in *The Castle of Perseverance*, fights against Wrath. What the *exemplum* in *Patience* chiefly does is to display some of those various passions which, in a man like Jonah, call for the control of patience. The poem vividly portrays and subtly discriminates the varieties of wrath that are 'evoked by hardship'. When God decides to spare Nineveh, for instance, Jonah's wrath takes the form of righteous indignation:

'I wyst wel, when I hade worded quatsoever I cowthe
To manace alle thise mody men that in this mote dwellez,
Wyth a prayer and a pyne thay myght her pese gete.'

(421–3)

> I knew very well that, when I had said everything I could to threaten all these proud men living in this place, they would be able to win a reprieve with a prayer and a single act of penance.

As in the scene in *Piers Plowman* (B XIII) where Will is half restrained by Patience from speaking his mind about the corrupt Friar, patience is here shown to entail an ability to suffer even the wickedness of 'mody men'. Both poets recognize the frequently dubious origins, in such cases, of righteous indignation (resentment, wounded vanity, envy); and both contrast this human indignation, comically, with the majestic long-suffrance of God the creator and redeemer. The virtue of patience, as Chaucer's Parson says, 'maketh a man lyk to God' (X 661).

Only a narrow and perverse idea of literature would attempt to deflect a reader from responding directly to the central exemplary meaning of a work such as *Patience*. Talk of 'fictional narrators' and the like, though not entirely unjustified, seems trivial and distracting here. *Patience* has the power of bringing its moral idea to life. A vivid and well-centred *exemplum* such as this can still 'edify the ignorant', by helping us to understand what familiar but faded moral terms like 'patience' can really mean; and that is not a matter of merely historical—or merely 'literary'—interest.

5 The survival of Middle English literature

Most readers of Middle English, even today, are more interested in English literature than they are in the Middle Ages; and for them the natural way to understand Langland or Chaucer is to relate them not to their medieval predecessors but to their modern successors. It seems appropriate, therefore, that this book should end with some discussion of the relationship between Middle and Modern English literature. I shall take as the starting-point a passage of Puttenham's *Arte of English Poesie*, published in 1589, from a chapter headed 'Who in any age have been the most commended writers in our English poesy, and the author's censure given upon them' (Book I Chapter XXXI). The Elizabethan author's discussion of the 'most commended writers' of the English Middle Ages deserves to be quoted in its entirety:

> I will not reach above the time of King Edward the Third and Richard the Second [1327–77–99] for any that wrote in English metre, because before their times, by reason of the late Norman conquest, which had brought into this realm much alteration both of our language and laws, and therewithall a certain martial barbarousness, whereby the study of all good learning was so much decayed as long time after no man or very few entended to write in any laudable science: so as beyond that time there is little or nothing worth commendation to be found written in this art. And those of the first age were Chaucer and Gower, both of them, as I suppose, knights. After whom followed John Lydgate, the monk of Bury, and that nameless, who wrote the satire called *Piers Plowman*; next him followed Hardyng, the chronicler; then, in King Henry the Eighth's time, Skelton (I wot not for what great worthiness) surnamed the poet laureate. In the latter end of the same king's reign sprang up a new company of courtly makers, of whom Sir Thomas Wyatt the elder and Henry Earl of Surrey were the two chieftains, who having travelled into Italy, and there tasted the sweet and stately measures and style of the Italian poesy, as novices newly crept out of the schools of Dante, Ariosto, and Petrarch, they greatly polished our rude and homely manner of vulgar

poesy from that it had been before, and for that cause may justly be said the first reformers of our English metre and style.[1]

Puttenham here strikes a note not to be heard in any medieval English vernacular writer: the excitement of belonging to a new and better age. In writing of the English past, he sees 'a certain martial barbarousness' and a 'rude and homely manner of vulgar poesy'—at least since the time of the Anglo-Saxons, for whom he evidently felt the vague veneration common in his day. In modern times, by contrast, he sees 'good learning', 'polish', and a 'reformed' metre and style. He does not explain the change; but his reference to the travels of Wyatt and Surrey in Italy chimes well with modern notions, derived from Burckhardt, of a European Renaissance originating in that country. The problems of the Renaissance and England's relation to it lie beyond the scope of this book; but Puttenham was certainly not alone when he claimed that English poetry had been reformed, if not reborn, in his century; and modern literary historians agree with him in looking to Italy for a chief source of the new 'sweet and stately measures and style' of Elizabethan verse. Chaucer, it is true, had also 'travelled into Italy'; but perhaps he is the exception that proves the rule.

It would be wrong, however, to suppose anything like a clean break between medieval and modern literature in the English Renaissance. English readers and writers of the early modern period are distinguished from their Italian and French contemporaries by their greater fidelity to old authors. The bibliographer E. P. Goldschmidt observes: 'a great proportion of the surviving writings of the Middle Ages were not only known but in current use and circulation continuously till about 1600; though to a diminishing degree in the latter half of the sixteenth century. The full eclipse and total oblivion of the "monkish" literature of the "Dark Ages" does not set in till the seventeenth century and the "Age of Reason"'.[2] Chaucer was, of course, outstandingly the most popular survivor. The debt of Spenser and Milton to Chaucer is well known; but there are many less obvious debts. Shakespeare's *Midsummer Night's Dream*, for instance, owes much to the *Knight's Tale*. Shakespeare also had a hand in a dramatic version of the same Tale, *The Two Noble Kinsmen*.[3] At the end of the seventeenth century, John Dryden modernized this and other Canterbury Tales in his *Fables* (1700). Gower was also quite widely read: Shakespeare's *Pericles* is based on a story by 'ancient Gower', who appears on stage as a Chorus; and Ben Jonson in his English Grammar takes many of his examples of correct English usage from *Confessio Amantis*. There are also countless obscurer instances of the same fidelity. Thus William Browne of Tavistock included Thomas Hoccleve's story of Jonathas and

Fellicula, modernized from Hoccleve's *Series*, in his *Shepheards Pipe* (1614). Following Spenser, who in the pastoral mode canonized Chaucer as 'Tityrus', Browne has one of his shepherds praise Hoccleve as 'scholar unto Tityrus':

> 'There are few such swains as he
> Nowadays for harmony.'

Bibliographical evidence points to the continued study of certain Middle English writers in the early modern period. Printed editions of Chaucer were especially frequent, from the incunabula of Caxton and Pynson to the edition of Thomas Speght (1598), which remained standard throughout the seventeenth century and was used by Dryden; but other Middle English writings also found their way into print: Gower's *Confessio Amantis* (Caxton 1483, Berthelette 1532 and 1554), Langland's *Piers Plowman* (Crowley 1550, Rogers 1561), Hilton's *Ladder of Perfection* (Wynkyn de Worde 1494, 1525 and 1533, Notary 1507, T. R. 1659), Lydgate's *Fall of Princes* (Pynson 1494 and 1527, Tottel 1554, Wayland *c.*1555), Malory's *Morte d'Arthur* (Caxton 1485, Wynkyn de Worde 1498 and 1529, Copland 1557, East *c.*1585, Stansby 1634), and Henryson's *Fables* (Charteris 1569/70, Bassandyne 1571, Smith 1577, Hart 1621), among others. Also, the habit of reading old manuscript copies persisted into the seventeenth century. At the beginning of the chapter from which I have just quoted, Puttenham refers to 'sundry records of books both printed *and written*'. Editors of Middle English texts have little occasion to record the many sixteenth- and seventeenth-century marginalia to be found in their medieval manuscripts. Some are mere marks of ownership, scribbles, or pen-trials; but others testify by comment or gloss to the fact that some reader in the age of Shakespeare or Milton has, for one reason or another, paid close attention to the ancient text. At the end of the autograph Durham Manuscript of Hoccleve's *Series*, for instance, 'Perlegi 1666' is written, in the hand of a chaplain to the Bishop of Durham. It is curious to think of a subject of Charles II 'reading through' such an obscure text from the age of Henry V. Some readers even went to the lengths of transcribing or commissioning their own written copies of medieval works which for some reason they were not able to possess in print. Thus, in the 1560s the Scotsman George Bannatyne transcribed (sometimes from printed sources) many medieval writings into a manuscript which is now one of the chief sources for older Scottish poetry. Similarly, the Percy Folio, a manuscript copied about the middle of the seventeenth century, preserves Middle English work which would otherwise have been lost. The Chester cycle of mystery plays survives more or less complete in five manuscript copies all of which date from between 1591 and 1607; and the two main witnesses to the long text of Julian of Norwich's mystical *Revelations* are manuscripts copied by Catholics in the mid-seventeenth century.

The interest of Chester people in their mystery cycle and of English recusants in old mystical writings shows how medieval texts could still continue to be *used* even as late as the seventeenth century, much as they had been used in their heyday, as texts for dramatic performance or devout meditation. Similarly, the treatises of the fifteenth-century lawyer Sir John Fortescue, *De Laudibus Legum Angliae* and *On the Governance of England*, were still being copied in the sixteenth and seventeenth centuries as living guides to English law and government. So, too, the courtly lyric poetry of Chaucer and his successors continued to be used for song and 'dalliance' in the earlier Tudor court—a continuity which Puttenham recognizes when he speaks of the 'new company of courtly makers' in the time of Henry VIII as successors to Chaucer and Gower. Sooner or later, however, these continuities were bound to be broken. New religious beliefs, new kinds of drama, new court fashions would progressively deprive Middle English texts of their original functions, and leave them to survive either as works of literature or as objects of antiquarian study.

Antiquarianism is, generally speaking, conspicuous by its absence in the Middle English period. The world 'old' itself, so often honorific in Anglo-Saxon, tends to depreciation in Middle English—Sir Gawain, expecting a smart Green Chapel, finds 'nobot an olde cave'—and there is little sign that old vernacular texts, any more than old buildings, were valued for their antiquity. According to the poet himself, Richard II asked Gower 'That to his hihe worthinesse/Som newe thing I scholde boke' (*Confessio Amantis* Prologue 50*–51*); and Chaucer, in the prologue to his *Sir Thopas*, apologizes because it is *old*: 'a rym I lerned longe agoon' (*Canterbury Tales* VII 709). As the 'newe thinges' of Chaucer and Gower themselves grew old, however, they were to depend largely for their survival upon an antiquarianism quite alien to their authors. Antiquarian interest in old vernacular writings hardly emerges before Tudor times; and it is closely associated from the first with another sentiment of which there is little trace in medieval writers: the sense of England. The Middle English *Song of Agincourt* expresses nationalistic hostility towards the French and patriotic pride in the English; but England as a place, with its own traditions linked to its own towns and rivers and seas, played little part in Middle English literature. It was the Tudor antiquarians and topographers such as John Leland, John Bale, and John Stow who first combined an interest in England with an interest in her old writers. Stow's two main works represent a typical combination of topographical and philological learning: an edition of Chaucer (1561) and a Survey of London (1598).

The same interest in England and her past which inspired men like Stow to collect and preserve old manuscripts led less learned men to conceive for the first time of 'English literature'. Puttenham's discussion of 'the most commended writers in our English poesy' may nowadays appear a not very sophisticated piece of literary history; but it displays a historical sense of continuity in English writings for which it would be hard to find a parallel in the Middle Ages. Whereas Dunbar's famous list of dead poets in the *Lament for the Makaris*, being concerned with the ahistorical fact of death, departs from chronological order and displays little sense of literary tradition, Puttenham traces the main line of English poetry from Chaucer and Gower to Wyatt and Surrey and beyond in a truly historical fashion, relating the laureate succession of poets to the better known chronology of monarchs: 'In the latter end of the same king's reign sprang up a new company of courtly makers . . .'. We see here the beginnings of a canonical history, and a historical canon, of English Literature with which we are still familiar: John Stevens, in his recent *Music and Poetry in the Early Tudor Court*, gives essentially the same account of the relation between Wyatt and Chaucer as does Puttenham.

One may say, then, that English Literature is in one sense a creation of the Tudor age, and that certain Middle English writers were incorporated into its canon and history posthumously. This chapter will return later to that process of incorporation; but first I want to explore further the reasons why the notion of English Literature developed when it did, and the implications of that development for the understanding of earlier writings.

The historian G. R. Elton has said that the most notable thing about Tudor polity was 'the emergence of a unitary and dynamic political structure involving rulers and ruled'; and it may well be that the emergence of a 'unitary and dynamic' national literature was an almost inevitable concomitant of that development towards political unity under Henry VII and his successors. There is, however, another factor of more particular relevance to literature, and that is the coming of the printing press. The first book to be printed in English was William Caxton's *History of Troy*, in 1473 or 1474; and this date has perhaps a better claim than any other to mark the beginning of the unitary and dynamic literary tradition. In some ways, as an earlier chapter suggested, the new technology of print made less immediate difference than might be supposed. The habit of reading poetry and prose, as against listening to them, had already spread widely through English society in the last centuries of the manuscript era; and the coming of print may be said to have done no more, in the fifteenth and sixteenth centuries, than accelerate that process. By producing more copies of texts more uniformly, however, the early printers greatly improved the chances that a given work would be read by contemporaries in different parts of England, and also that it would be preserved for posterity and consulted by later readers. It became less likely that a work would either pass unnoticed at the time of its composition or else fall into oblivion shortly thereafter, as happened to so many works in the age of manuscript. Sixteenth-century readers were in a much better position than their medieval predecessors to know both what their own contemporaries were writing and also what had been written in the past. What readers did not know was more and more what they did not want to know, not what they had simply lost or missed. A canon was in process of formation.

In the Middle Ages, the only literary canon known to readers was that of the Latin and (by repute) the Greek classics, a canon defined and transmitted by the schools.[4] If a vernacular writer imagined himself canonized—and few did—he could think only of joining the august company of classical writers. In the *Inferno*, Dante is received as a brother poet by Homer, Horace, Ovid, Lucan, and Virgil:

> They took me as a member of their company,
> So that I was a sixth among those great intellects.

(Inferno IV 101–2)

In a similar fashion, but more modestly, Chaucer tells his *Troilus* to

> kis the steppes, where as thow seest pace
> Virgile, Ovide, Omer, Lucan, and Stace.   (V 1791–2)

In the vernaculars, French, Italian, or English, there was no such canon. Chaucer had probably read more English poetry than used to be supposed; but his knowledge of both predecessors and contemporaries must have been extremely patchy. It was, in fact, impossible for any medieval writer to take a synoptic view of his own literature.

In this respect, a modern scholar has an advantage over Chaucer. In principle, one man can now know everything that survives of Middle English literature. Yet even if everything had survived, a synoptic view of literature in this period would remain elusive. The picture would still be fragmented and discontinuous. In the absence of a 'unitary and dynamic' tradition, early writers were largely dependent for vernacular precedent on what happened to survive and be available in their particular part of the country. Hence continuous sequences of development such as literary historians look for—one writer learning from, or reacting against, others—appear relatively rarely in medieval English literature; and such traditions, when they do appear, are usually associated with particular parts of the country. Medieval vernacular literature, like medieval society, was in fact profoundly *regional* in character—quite different in this respect from medieval Latin, which had a standard language, international circulation, and a classical canon behind it. Literary historians will trace sequences of historically related texts in the vernacular corpus; but even the most impressive of these falls short of full national status. It may be argued that the homilies of Ælfric, composed in the standard literary language of Wessex during the short-lived period of its national hegemony, did achieve national status for a time; but after the Norman Conquest that tradition of English prose assumes a markedly regional character: it is only in the west, and especially in the Worcester region, that Old English prose continued to be copied, and it is in the same region that *Ancrene Wisse* and the 'Katherine Group' texts were composed.

To call Modern English literature, by contrast with Middle English, 'unitary' may seem a questionable assertion. Was there not as much diversity in English writings of around 1800 as there was around 1200? Indeed, was there not *more* diversity? The diversity, however, is of a different sort. Jane Austen and Wordsworth wrote very different kinds of work; but although they lived in widely separated parts of the country, they both belonged to the same literary scene. Their works, that is, can be related to each other as parts of a single pattern, however complex, of shared or disputed traditions. If they differ, they do so, in the last analysis, deliberately; and literary historians can therefore make sense of their differences—by contrasting, say, their attitudes to Dr Johnson and other eighteenth-century predecessors. But the relationship between *Sir Gawain* and *Troilus* is in this respect unlike the relationship between *Pride and Prejudice* and *Lyrical Ballads*. There is no evidence that the *Gawain*-poet even knew of Chaucer's existence; and, although Chaucer did know something of alliterative verse, the allusion by the Parson in the *Canterbury Tales* displays a provincial attitude typical of his time:

> 'But trusteth wel, I am a Southren man,
> I kan nat geeste "rum, ram, ruf," by lettre.'   (X 42–3)
> *geeste*] tell stories

These verses have tempted some literary historians to suppose that alliterative and syllabic verse were rivals in the fourteenth century, rather like free and traditional verse in the early twentieth; but the Parson's words point in a different direction. He rejects alliterative verse, not because he regards it as the wrong way to do English poetry, but because he is a *Southern* man—and Southern men neither understand nor like that sort of thing. Alliterative verse was for him in effect a foreign tradition. This attitude of the Parson is typical, if not of Chaucer himself, then certainly of his period.

It will be obvious that the arrival of printing in the century after Chaucer must have told in the long run against such regionalism. The new technology could not fail to foster a more unitary awareness of the English literary tradition. But the matter is better understood in a broader context. It is a curious fact, often noted, that many of the discoveries and developments, literary and otherwise, now regarded as characteristic of the modern age can be shown by scholars to have occurred already in the Middle Ages. Indeed, some of them, such as the rediscovery of Greek, seem to have occurred several times. And it is there that the difference lies. Once a discovery or development is registered in printed form, it is normally secured for posterity. Posterity may of course reject or reverse it; but they are unlikely simply not to know that it has occurred. In the manuscript age, on the other hand, it frequently happened that the same development occurred several times, each time independently. Ground won—in the natural sciences, in exploration, in Bible translation, or in scholarship— was easily lost, and then perhaps won again, and again lost. There can be little doubt that printing did more than anything else to change this situation, as Elizabeth Eisenstein argues in her book *The Printing Press as an Agent of Change*. Speaking of Classical scholarship (an essential element in most definitions of the Renaissance), she says this: 'The recovery of ancient languages followed the same pattern as the recovery of ancient texts. A process which had hitherto been intermittent became subject to continuous, incremental change. Once a finding could be permanently secured by being registered in print, the way was paved for an unending series of discoveries and for the systematic development of investigatory techniques'.[5]

This fundamental contrast between the 'intermittent' culture of the manuscript age and the 'continuous, incremental' culture of the age of print can be illustrated by a brief consideration of the early history of standard written English—itself a matter of considerable importance for literature. It is sometimes suggested that medieval scribes had no notion of conforming to any standard when they wrote vernacular texts. But it cannot be literally true that scribes wrote as they pleased, for such writings would have been unintelligible; and in fact some of them can be shown to have achieved a degree of consistent regularity in spellings and forms which is actually *greater* than we normally find in printed books until the later seventeenth century. Where a number of such manuscripts written by different hands agree together, we must suppose that the scribes in question are conforming to some accepted standard of written English. Such is certainly the case with those Anglo-Saxon scribes of the tenth and eleventh centuries who conformed to the Winchester standard of Late West Saxon. These men produced copies of vernacular prose and verse so consistent in orthography that modern editors, producing normalized texts for beginners, can achieve complete uniformity with very few changes. There is no reason, after all, why a well-drilled scribe should not set down letters as consistently as a well-drilled printer's compositor. The difference is simply that the Late West Saxon standard did not *last*; and although the West Midland successors of Ælfric developed a new literary standard of their own, the so-called 'AB dialect' found so regularly in some manuscripts of *Ancrene Wisse* and the Katherine Group, that did not last either. Such standards are, in fact, typically 'intermittent' achievements of the manuscript age. It was only when yet another written standard, the so-called 'Chancery Standard' developed by fifteenth-century scribes and clerks, was taken up and permanently secured by the first printers that England acquired a unitary language for its literature. That language has, of course, not remained static since the time of Caxton; but its history has been *continuous*. A modern reader can work back via Milton, Spenser, and Malory to Chaucer and Gower, without encountering any break in the linguistic chain. Chaucer and Gower are therefore more accessible to us than some Middle English (not to speak of Old English) writers were to them.

It is no coincidence that Puttenham's list of 'the most commended writers in our English poesy' includes no Middle English writers unfortunate enough to employ a form of English remote from that which the London printers were to canonize. Sixteenth-century readers accustomed to the language of the Tyndale and Coverdale Bibles, the Book of Common Prayer, or Foxe's Book of Martyrs, would have relatively little difficulty with a printed text of the *Canterbury Tales*, *Confessio Amantis*, or Lydgate's *Fall of Princes*; but no printer in his senses would have offered them an edition of *Sir Gawain* or *Pearl*, simply because of the difficulties which the poet's North-Western dialect presented. English literature, as it emerged in the age of printing, was not itself tied to any particular region—on the contrary, it was in essence national—but there was a strong regional bias in the retrospective selection of those Middle English writers judged to be worth commendation by men like Puttenham.

There is, then, a distinction between those Middle English works which were admitted into the canon in the early modern period and those which were left to the curiosity of the antiquarian reader. In so far as the distinction is one of literary quality, a present-day student of literature may be content to accept the resulting selection; but one of the chief themes of modern criticism of medieval literature has been to press the claims of those works of real quality which were originally excluded from the canon for contingent reasons of unacceptable dialect or simple unavailability. The most conspicuous case is the uncanonical masterpiece *Sir Gawain and the Green Knight*. This survives in a single manuscript copy. There is some evidence that it continued to be read in the North West Midlands up to the early sixteenth century; but after that it seems to have been forgotten even in its own dialect area. The surviving manuscript passed into the hands of a Yorkshire antiquary, Henry Savile (1568–1617), and then to Sir Robert Cotton, and then eventually to the British Library, where it still remains. No part of *Sir Gawain* appeared in print until as late as 1824, when Richard Price quoted one passage (lines 20–36) in his revision of Thomas Warton's *History of English Poetry*; and the whole poem was not made available in print until 1839, when it was published by the Bannatyne Club, with the encouragement of Sir Walter Scott. The Early English Text Society produced an edition in 1864, since when the poem has been frequently edited; but even today knowledge of the poem is largely restricted, for linguistic reasons, to academic circles. It is, by comparison with Chaucer's *Canterbury Tales*, still only dubiously canonical.

The history of the survival and revival of *Sir Gawain* is typical of those many Middle English works which, for one reason or another, failed to establish a place in the canon when it was first formed in Tudor times. The three main works of Early Middle English literature, for instance, became available only in the nineteenth century, when Victorian philologists produced printed editions: Stevenson's *Owl and The Nightingale* in 1838, Madden's *Brut* in 1847, and Morton's *Ancren Riwle* in 1853. Almost the whole corpus of medieval alliterative verse went underground in the same way. The standard language of printed literature is the language of the 'Southren man'; and since most 'rum, ram, ruf' was composed up north or away in the west, it is not surprising that so little found its way into print. The most conspicuous exception is the 'satire called *Piers Plowman*', itself probably written in London, for which Puttenham found a place in his list. Langland's reputation as a satirist especially of popish abuses, 'crying out against the works of darkness', commended him to the Puritan printer Crowley, and also to readers such as Spenser and Milton; but otherwise very little alliterative verse remained available—perhaps only the alliterative *Morte Arthure*, half turned into prose by Sir Thomas Malory and printed by Caxton as Book V of his *Morte d'Arthur*.

This broad difference between those Middle English works which survived as part of the literary canon and those which had to be rescued from obscurity by nineteenth-century scholars is a matter of more than merely historical interest. It still introduces distortions into our view of the period. The tradition of most commended writers traced by Puttenham no longer enjoys the absolute advantage it once had, especially from about 1660 until the nineteenth century. The merits of *Sir Gawain*, and *Pearl*, and *Patience*, and *Winner and Waster*, and even *The Owl and the Nightingale* and *Ancrene Wisse* are now quite justly appreciated, even in the face of considerable linguistic difficulties. Quite apart from linguistic difficulties, however, these non-canonical works continue to present a special challenge to criticism—a challenge which arises precisely from the fact of their absence from the general canon throughout the greater part of the modern period. In the case of the 'most commended writers', above all in the case of Chaucer, we can draw upon the responses of many generations of English readers and writers. Caroline Spurgeon's monumental book, *Five Hundred Years of Chaucer Criticism and Allusion*, recording these responses, has the effect of showing Chaucer through Tudor, Restoration, eighteenth-century, and Romantic eyes;[6] and the way his work was received, especially by fellow-poets, in those different periods reveals, often, precisely those sides of Chaucer's work which we are least well-placed to see in our particular period. Spenser and Milton, for instance, both direct attention to the unfinished and nowadays neglected *Squire's Tale*: Spenser by his continuation of the Tale in Book IV of the *Faerie Queene*, Milton by his allusion to Chaucer as

> him that left half-told
> The story of Cambuscan bold,
> Of Camball, and of Algarsife,
> And who had Canace to wife,
> That owned the virtuous ring and glass,
> And of the wondrous horse of brass,
> On which the Tartar king did ride.   (*Il Penseroso* 109–15)

That is not our Chaucer. Critics in the later age of the novel were even to suggest that the poet deliberately aborted the *Squire's Tale*, as he did *Sir Thopas*, out of sheer impatience with its insipid marvels. Yet a more attentive and unprejudiced reading, such as Milton may prompt, will put that suggestion out of court. Consider the Squire's description of the 'wondrous horse of brass':

> For it so heigh was, and so brood and long,
> So wel proporcioned for to been strong,
> Right as it were a steede of Lumbardye;
> Therwith so horsly, and so quyk of ye,
> As it a gentil Poilleys courser were.   (V 191–5)

Poilleys] Apulian

A later poet, Leigh Hunt, rightly said that this horse 'is copied from the life. You might pat him and feel his brazen muscles'.[7]

Poets' modernizations of Chaucer also reveal a great deal, both about their own age and also about Chaucer himself in relation to that age. The Preface to John Dryden's *Fables* is generally recognized as one of the three classics of pre-academic Chaucer criticism (the others are William Blake's *Descriptive Catalogue* and Matthew Arnold's essay 'The Study of Poetry');

but the versions from the *Canterbury Tales* which it introduces are equally illuminating. 'I prefer in our countryman, far above all his other stories, the noble poem of Palamon and Arcite, which is of the epique kind, and perhaps not much inferior to the *Ilias* or the *Aeneis*: the story is more pleasing than either of them, the manners as perfect, the diction as poetical, the learning as deep and various, and the disposition full as artful'. In an earlier chapter I argued that the *Knight's Tale* differs from its Italian original in *not* aspiring to the 'epique kind'; but Dryden knew what heroic poetry was—he had written it—and his version of Chaucer's poem displays that 'nobility' which modern readers easily miss. Using the old black-letter edition of Speght, Dryden does not always get things right; but his rendering, for instance, of Theseus' merciful treatment of the two young lovers preserves in its own fashion the true weight and dignity of Chaucer's Duke:

> He shook his head,
> And softly sighing to himself he said:
> 'Curse on th'unpardoning prince, whom tears can draw
> To no remorse; who rules by lion's law;
> And, deaf to prayers, by no submission bowed,
> Rends all alike, the penitent and proud.'
> At this with look serene he raised his head;
> Reason resumed her place, and passion fled.
> Then thus aloud he spoke: 'The power of love,
> In earth, and seas, and air, and heaven above,
> Rules unresisted, with an awful nod;
> By daily miracles declared a god . . .'

(Palamon and Arcite II 342–53)

Having lived under the Stuart monarchy, Dryden could still appreciate something of the 'awful' power of a Duke or a God to grant or withhold favour at a nod; and his version recalls us from the democratic familiarities of much modern commentary to a truer sense of what, for a subject of Richard II, the authority of Theseus must have meant.

Chaucer is quite exceptional in the amount of attention paid him by his successors. Writers such as Langland, Gower, Lydgate, Hoccleve, and Malory attracted much less comment. Yet they too can be understood in relation to that subsequent tradition of English literature for which they have been, like Chaucer but much more modestly, continuing presences. When the Tudor printer Berthelette speaks, in his edition of *Confessio Amantis* (1532), of Gower as a model of good, unaffected English, who can teach a modern writer to 'wryte counnyngly and to garnysshe his sentencis in our vulgar tonge', or when Thomas Warton, in his *History of English*

Poetry (1774–81), speaks of his 'critical cultivation of his native language', these testimonies display Gower's relation to the ideal of plain, correct English beloved of some Tudor and many eighteenth-century writers. He is perhaps the only Middle English writer, in fact, to whom the later ideal of 'correctness' could be applied without embarrassment. Nor is it without significance as an index of Romantic taste, on the other hand, that Coleridge classed him (with disapproval) among 'the lengthy poets' and referred to him as 'the almost worthless Gower'.

Modern criticism of Chaucer and Gower and the other canonical poets generally pays little attention to these pre-academic testimonies; but their true value can be judged from those cases where they are not available. How much would we have learned about *Sir Gawain* if Dr Johnson or John Keats had been able to read it? What would Ben Jonson have made of *Winner and Waster*? Or Thomas Traherne of *Pearl*? Or John Milton of Laȝamon's *Brut*? The impossibility of answering such questions contributes to a certain blankness in our reception of these works—a failure confidently to set them in relation to the main tradition of English literature. Most of them have by now been available for more than a century. Admittedly, they have not been entirely ignored by creative artists in modern times. Indeed, they may be said to have prompted more creative response than Chaucer has. Holman Hunt drew a frontispiece for Gollancz's edition of *Pearl* (an interesting conjunction); Igor Stravinsky and Benjamin Britten, among others, have set Middle English lyrics to music, and Britten has also set the Chester play of Abraham and Isaac in his Canticle II; W. B. Yeats adapted the Rawlinson lyric 'I am of Ireland' in his *Words for Music Perhaps*; T. S. Eliot claimed to have derived the versification of *Murder in the Cathedral* from the moral play *Everyman*; and W. H. Auden wrote alliterative verse in *The Age of Anxiety*. Yet it cannot be claimed that the efforts of editors, critics, musicians, and writers have quite succeeded in restoring the best of these non-canonical works to their proper place besides the most commended writers. The fate of the alliterative tradition in the twentieth century provides a demonstration of this. It is understandable that during the eighteenth and nineteenth centuries alliterative verse should seem a form without a future, even to sympathetic scholars such as Thomas Warton or W. W. Skeat. The principles of syllable-count, regularly recurring ictus, and end-rhyme, so deeply entrenched in the poetry of Pope and Tennyson, did not encourage such poets to experiment with a kind of verse which varied the number of syllables at will, spaced the ictus irregularly, and substituted head-rhyme for end-rhyme. It required a considerable adjustment to accept the rhythms of such poetry as verse rhythms, and to hear alliteration as a formal requirement, not an overdone expressive option. As the nineteenth century progressed, however, habits of syllable-count and rhyme which had prevailed for so long began to be questioned; and poets such as Gerard Manley Hopkins began to experiment with alternative ways of writing poetry. At this point one would have expected alliterative verse, already available in modern editions and well understood by scholars such as Skeat, to re-enter the mainstream of English poetry, as a living alternative to rhymed verse, as it had been in Chaucer's time. But this has not happened. No one actually acquainted with medieval alliterative verse seriously supposes that Hopkins wrote anything similar. His search for an alternative tradition did lead him to look at Langland; but he found *Piers* disappointing: 'I am reading that famous poem and am coming to the conclusion that it is not worth reading' (letter to Bridges, 18 October 1882). In the present century, W. H. Auden has written correct alliterative verse; but this Alliterative Revival, if it may be called such, has not succeeded in breaking out from the academic and antiquarian circles to which knowledge of the form has for so long been confined. Auden, it is relevant to recall, read English at Oxford.

The future of Middle English literature, including that of alliterative verse, can only be guessed at. It is unlikely that many major texts remain to be rediscovered. Small things keep turning up; but the only big discovery since the Second World War to compare with the pre-War finding of *The Book of Margery Kempe*, the alliterative *Mum and the Sothsegger*, or the pre-Caxton text of Malory, is the *Equatorie of the Planetis*—and that only if the editor's attribution to Chaucer is accepted.[8] The record will certainly remain fragmentary (barring time-travel) and continue to frustrate literary historians. On the other hand, editors, palaeographers, philologists, and lexicographers still have a big contribution to make to the understanding of the surviving texts, as have historians of medieval thought and society. Increasingly exact historical and philological understanding of the old texts should not preclude—indeed, should prompt and quicken—fresh critical assessment. Middle English literature is not the same in the twentieth century as it was in the nineteenth; and in the twenty-first it will no doubt be different again. Just how different it will be depends very largely, I suspect, on the future fate of that 'continuous, incremental' literary tradition which still looks back to Puttenham and to those medieval writers accepted as canonical in Puttenham's day. For it is not only devotees of the Middle Ages who object to the notion of Chaucer as the father of English poetry (Dryden's phrase); and it may be that the Chaucer tradition—that kind of poetry, written in that kind of English, in that kind of metre, printed in that kind of book—will face increasing challenge in the future from rival traditions which do not recognize the language of the Authorized Version as their English. It would be surprising, after all, if the tradition of Chaucer, Milton, and Tennyson were to suffer no challenge in an age where English is a world language and England no longer a world power. Perhaps, therefore, future readers will be able to look more dispassionately at Middle English literature, and future writers will discover kinships with predecessors now hardly known outside the universities.

Notes

Chapter 1

1. For an account of the language in the Middle English period, see Barbara M. H. Strang, *A History of English* (London, 1970), Chapters III, IV and V.
2. On Anglo-Norman literature see M. D. Legge, *Anglo-Norman Literature and its Background* (Oxford, 1963).
3. See especially R. W. Southern, *The Making of the Middle Ages* (London, 1953).
4. See C. H. Haskins, *The Renaissance of the Twelfth Century* (Cambridge, Mass., 1927).
5. See W. P. Ker, *Epic and Romance: Essays on Medieval Literature* (London, 1897, reissued New York, 1957).
6. Cited by V. Erlich, *Russian Formalism* (The Hague, Paris, 1969), p. 183.
7. Northrop Frye, *Anatomy of Criticism* (Princeton, 1957), p. 74.
8. G. Genette, *Figures* (Paris, 1966), p. 146.
9. A Modern English translation of this Latin version may be found in A. S. Preminger, O. B. Hardison, and K. Kerrane, *Classical and Medieval Literary Criticism: Translations and Interpretations* (New York, 1974).
10. *Apology for Poetry*, ed. G. Shepherd (London, 1965), pp. 123–4. Shepherd's Introduction is especially valuable.
11. Jonson's remark is reported in his *Conversations with William Drummond of Hawthornden* (1619).
12. John of Garland's *Parisiana Poetria* is edited, with translation and commentary, by T. Lawler (New Haven and London, 1974). For other medieval Latin arts of poetry, see E. Faral (ed.), *Les Arts Poétiques du XIIe et du XIIIe Siècle* (Paris, 1924).
13. See W. Wetherbee, *Platonism and Poetry in the Twelfth Century* (Princeton, 1972).
14. Ed. Vinaver, p. xv.
15. *Lyrical Ballads*, ed. R. L. Brett and A. R. Jones (London, 1963), p. 237.

16. Cited by H. J. Chaytor, *From Script to Print* (Cambridge, 1945), p. 86. Chaytor's chapter 'Prose and Translation' is useful.

17. Ed. Shepherd, p. 102.

18. Cited by C. Grayson, 'Dante and the Renaissance', in C. P. Brand, K. Foster, and U. Limentani (eds.), *Italian Studies Presented to E. R. Vincent* (Cambridge, 1962), p. 69.

19. On Mazzoni, see B. Hathaway, *The Age of Criticism: The Late Renaissance in Italy* (Ithaca, N.Y., 1962), pp. 76–8. See generally Hathaway's Chapter 4, 'Were Empedocles and Lucretius Poets?'.

Chapter 2

1. The Vercelli Book, in the cathedral library of Vercelli, Italy; the Exeter Book, in the cathedral library of Exeter; the Cædmon Manuscript, MS Junius 11 in the Bodleian Library, Oxford; and the *Beowulf* Manuscript, Cotton Vitellius A xv in the British Library, London.

2. On oral composition, see A. B. Lord, *The Singer of Tales* (Cambridge, Mass., 1960).

3. See M. T. Clanchy, *From Memory to Written Record: England 1066–1307* (London, 1979).

4. See Alfred's Preface to the Anglo-Saxon version of Gregory's *Cura Pastoralis*: Modern English translation in *English Historical Documents: c.500–1042*, ed. D. Whitelock (London, 1968), pp. 818–19.

5. E. J. Dobson proposes John of Lingen as the author of *Ancrene Wisse* in *The Origins of 'Ancrene Wisse'* (Oxford, 1976).

6. On Chaucer's official career, see F. R. H. du Boulay, 'The Historical Chaucer', in D. S. Brewer (ed.), *Geoffrey Chaucer* (Writers and their Background, London, 1974), pp. 33–57.

7. Bonaventure, *In Primum Librum Sententiarum*, proem, quaest. iv. Printed in *Opera* (Quaracchi ed.), i (1882), p. 14 col. 2; cited by M. B. Parkes, 'The Influence of the Concepts of *Ordinatio* and *Compilatio* on the Development of the Book', in J. J. G. Alexander and M. T. Gibson (eds.), *Medieval Learning and Literature: Essays Presented to R. W. Hunt* (Oxford, 1976), pp. 127–8.

8. Ed. Vinaver, p. 726.

9. Translations of *La Divina Commedia* are taken throughout from *The Divine Comedy: A New Verse Translation*, by C. H. Sisson (Manchester, 1980).

10. See K. Sisam, *Studies in the History of Old English Literature* (Oxford, 1953), p. 23.

11. Colin Morris, *The Discovery of the Individual 1050–1200* (London,

1972), p. 158. See also W. Ullmann, *The Individual and Society in the Middle Ages* (London, 1967), especially pp. 104 ff.

12. E. R. Curtius, *European Literature and the Latin Middle Ages*, trans. W. R. Trask (London, 1953), Excursus XVII: 'Mention of the Author's Name in Medieval Literature'.

13. On the acrostic, see W. W. Skeat's introduction to his edition of the *Testament of Love*, *Chaucerian and Other Pieces* (Oxford, 1897), pp. xix-xx.

14. Ed. F. J. Furnivall, in *Hoccleve's Minor Poems*, E.E.T.S., e.s. 61 (1892).

15. On Langland as Long Wille, see G. Kane, *Piers Plowman: The Evidence for Authorship* (London, 1965), Chapter IV.

16. For a detailed study of this passage, see E. T. Donaldson, *Piers Plowman: The C-Text and Its Poet* (New Haven, 1949), Chapter VII.

17. *Sawles Warde* lines 144–8, in J. A. W. Bennett and G. V. Smithers (eds.) *Early Middle English Verse and Prose* (Oxford, 1968).

18. The arts of second rhetoric are edited by E. Langlois, *Recueil d'Arts de Seconde Rhétorique* (Paris, 1902).

19. *Wars of Alexander*, ed. W. W. Skeat, E. E. T. S., e.s. 47 (1886), lines 4806–7.

20. Reproduced in G. Mathew, *The Court of Richard II* (London, 1968), Plate 15.

Chapter 3

1. For the duck-rabbit see p. 4 of E. H. Gombrich's seminal book, *Art and Illusion: A Study in the Psychology of Pictorial Representation* (London, 1960).

2. See W. P. Ker, *Form and Style in Poetry* (London, 1928), pp. 64–79. For selections from the *Teseida* in Modern English, see N. Havely, *Chaucer's Boccaccio* (Cambridge, 1980).

3. For editions, see Bibliography. Selected mystery plays in A. C. Cawley (ed.), *The Wakefield Pageants of the Towneley Cycle* (Manchester, 1958), and R. G. Thomas (ed.), *Ten Miracle Plays* (London, 1966). The best literary studies are: V. A. Kolve, *The Play Called Corpus Christi* (Stanford, 1966), and R. Woolf, *The English Mystery Plays* (London, 1972).

4. *Everyman* is edited by A. C. Cawley (Manchester, 1961), *The Castle of Perseverance* by M. Eccles in *The Macro Plays*, E.E.T.S., o.s. 262 (1969). A general study is R. Potter, *The English Morality Play* (London, 1975).

5. On medieval lyrics generally, see P. Dronke, *The Medieval Lyric* (London, 1968). I quote here from R. T. Davies's anthology,

Medieval English Lyrics (London, 1963). On secular lyric, see John Stevens, *Music and Poetry in the Early Tudor Court* (London, 1961). On religious lyric, see D. Gray, *Themes and Images in the Medieval English Religious Lyric* (London, 1972), and R. Woolf, *The English Religious Lyric in the Middle Ages* (Oxford, 1968).

6. An anthology of French poems in *formes fixes*, with music, may be found in N. Wilkins, *One Hundred Ballades, Rondeaux and Virelais from the Late Middle Ages* (Cambridge, 1969).

7. R. L. Greene's book (2nd ed., Oxford, 1977) provides the best discussion of the medieval carol, together with a full collection of texts.

8. See H. Delahaye, *The Legends of the Saints*, trans. D. Attwater (London, 1962).

9. For the *Gest of Robyn Hode*, see R. B. Dobson and J. Taylor, *Rymes of Robyn Hood* (London, 1976), a study and anthology of greenwood verse.

10. For an anthology of English specimens, see B. Boyd (ed.), *The Middle English Miracles of the Virgin* (San Marino, Cal., 1964).

11. On romance, see E. Auerbach, *Mimesis*, trans. W. R. Trask (New York, 1957), Chapter 6; John Stevens, *Medieval Romance* (London, 1973); and E. Vinaver, *The Rise of Romance* (Oxford, 1971). Also D. Mehl, *The Middle English Romances of the Thirteenth and Fourteenth Centuries* (London, 1968); and the anthology *Medieval English Romances*, ed. A. V. C. Schmidt and N. Jacobs (London, 1980).

12. Compare the excellent discussion of narrative speed, duration, and distance in G. Genette, *Narrative Discourse*, trans. J. E. Lewin (Oxford, 1980), Chapters 2 and 4.

13. Faral, *Arts Poétiques*, p. 203.

14. The best study is P. Nykrog, *Les Fabliaux* (Copenhagen, 1957). English discussions in C. Muscatine, *Chaucer and the French Tradition* (Berkeley, Cal., 1957), and D. S. Brewer, 'The Fabliaux', in B. Rowland (ed.), *Companion to Chaucer Studies* (New York, 1968), pp. 247–67. For specimens, with translations, see L. D. Benson and T. M. Andersson (eds.), *The Literary Context of Chaucer's Fabliaux* (Indianapolis and New York, 1971).

15. For Virgil's wheel, see Faral, *Arts Poétiques*, p. 87.

16. On Marie and the Breton lay, see R. S. Loomis (ed.), *Arthurian Literature in the Middle Ages* (Oxford, 1959), Chapter 11.

17. Cited from J-T. Welter, *L'Exemplum dans la Littérature Religieuse et Didactique du Moyen Age* (Paris, 1927), p. 68. Welter's is still the best study of *exempla*.

Chapter 4

1. For an introductory study, see J. MacQueen, *Allegory* (London, 1970). C. S. Lewis's *Allegory of Love* (Oxford, 1936) retains its value. More advanced studies are: Angus Fletcher, *Allegory: The Theory of a Symbolic Mode* (Ithaca, New York, 1964); D. W. Robertson, *A Preface to Chaucer* (Princeton, 1962); and R. Tuve, *Allegorical Imagery: Some Mediaeval Books and their Posterity* (Princeton, 1966).

2. From Coleridge's *Statesman's Manual*, cited in the useful collection of observations on allegory in C. Butler and A. D. S. Fowler, *Topics in Criticism* (London, 1971), No. 198.

3. Aquinas, *Summa Theologica* I q.1 a.10; Bonaventure, *Breviloquium* Prologue 6.

4. Text from J. A. Burrow (ed.), *English Verse 1300–1500* (London, 1977).

5. See M. Quilligan, *The Language of Allegory* (Ithaca, New York, 1979).

6. E. H. Gombrich, *Meditations on a Hobby Horse* (London, 1963), 'The Cartoonist's Armoury'.

7. See Curtius, *European Literature and the Latin Middle Ages*, Chapter 16: 'The Book as Symbol'.

8. Alanus de Insulis, in *The Oxford Book of Medieval Latin Verse*, ed. F. J. E. Raby (Oxford, 1959), No. 242.

9. Cited from *The Latin Works of Dante* (Temple Classics, London, 1904), pp. 347–8. The authenticity of this letter has been questioned.

10. Cited by Welter, *L'Exemplum*, p. 77. On *exempla* in sermons, see also G. R. Owst, *Literature and Pulpit in Medieval England* (Cambridge, 1933, reissued Oxford, 1961), Chapter IV.

11. See especially S. Wenzel, *The Sin of Sloth* (Chapel Hill, N.C., 1967).

12. For the (indirect) influence of Peraldus on the *Parson's Tale*, see S. Wenzel, *Traditio* 27 (1971) 433–53, and 30 (1974) 351–78. For his influence on Dante, see Wenzel, *Modern Language Review* 60 (1965) 529–33.

13. Faral, *Arts Poétiques*, p. 150.

14. Humbert de Romans, *De Habundancia Exemplorum*, cited by Welter, *L'Exemplum*, p. 73.

15. The comments quoted may be found in the Everyman translation (London, 1930), Vol. II pp. 334 and 343.

Chapter 5

1. Ed. G. Gregory Smith, *Elizabethan Critical Essays* (Oxford, 1904), Vol. II pp. 62–3.

2. E. P. Goldschmidt, *Medieval Texts and their First Appearance in Print* (London, 1943), p. 2.

3. See Ann Thompson, *Shakespeare's Chaucer* (Liverpool, 1978).

4. See Curtius, *European Literature and the Latin Middle Ages*, pp. 256–72.

5. E. Eisenstein, *The Printing Press as an Agent of Change* (Cambridge, 1979), p. 224. I am particularly indebted to this book in the present chapter.

6. C. F. E. Spurgeon, *Five Hundred Years of Chaucer Criticism and Allusion 1357–1900* (Cambridge, 1925, reissued New York, 1960). More recent collections of Chaucer criticism are J. A. Burrow (ed.), *Geoffrey Chaucer: A Critical Anthology* (London, 1969); and D. S. Brewer (ed.), *Chaucer, The Critical Heritage* (London, 1978).

7. *Imagination and Fancy* (1844), p. 16.

8. Printed for the first time by D. J. Price, *The Equatorie of the Planetis* (Cambridge, 1955).

Bibliography

Anthologies

Bennett, J. A. W., and Smithers, G. V. (eds.), *Early Middle English Verse and Prose*, Clarendon Press, Oxford, 1968.

Burrow, J. A. (ed.), *English Verse 1300–1500* (Longman Annotated Anthologies of English Verse), Longman, London and New York, 1977.

Davies, R. T. (ed.), *Medieval English Lyrics: A Critical Anthology*, Faber and Faber, London, 1963.

Sisam, C., and Sisam, K. (eds.), *The Oxford Book of Medieval English Verse*, Clarendon Press, Oxford, 1970.

Sisam, K. (ed.), *Fourteenth Century Verse and Prose*, Clarendon Press, Oxford, 1921.

Texts

Ancrene Wisse, Parts 6 and 7, ed. G. Shepherd (Nelson's Medieval and Renaissance Library), Nelson, London, 1959.

Chaucer, G., *Works*, ed. F. N. Robinson, 2nd edn., Houghton Mifflin, Boston, 1957.

Chester Mystery Cycle, vol. i, ed. R. M. Lumiansky and David Mills, E.E.T.S. s.s. 3, 1974.

Clanvowe, J., *Works*, ed. V. J. Scattergood, Brewer, Cambridge, 1975.

Cleanness, ed. J. J. Anderson, Manchester University Press, Manchester and New York, 1977.

Cloud of Unknowing, ed. Phyllis Hodgson, E.E.T.S. o.s. 218, 1944.

Dunbar, W., *Poems*, ed. James Kinsley, Clarendon Press, Oxford, 1979.

Everyman, ed. A. C. Cawley, Manchester University Press, Manchester, 1961.

Gest Hystoriale of the Destruction of Troy, ed. D. Donaldson and G. A. Panton, E.E.T.S. o.s. 39 and 56, 1869 and 1874.

Gower, J., *English Works*, ed. G. C. Macaulay, E.E.T.S. e.s. 81 and 82, 1900 and 1901.

Guy of Warwick, ed. J. Zupitza, E.E.T.S. e.s. 42, 49 and 59, 1883, 1887 and 1891.

Havelok, ed. W. W. Skeat, 2nd edn., revised K. Sisam, Clarendon Press, Oxford, 1915.

Henryson, R., *Poems*, ed. D. Fox, Clarendon Press, Oxford, 1981.

Hoccleve, T., *Regement of Princes*, ed. F. J. Furnivall, E.E.T.S. e.s. 72, 1897.

James I of Scotland, *The Kingis Quair*, ed. J. Norton-Smith (Clarendon Medieval and Tudor Series), Clarendon Press, Oxford, 1971.

Laȝamon, *Brut*, ed. G. L. Brook and R. F. Leslie, E.E.T.S. o.s. 250 and 277, 1963 and 1978.

Langland, W., *Piers Plowman*, B Text, ed. A. V. C. Schmidt (Everyman Library), Dent Dutton, London and New York, 1978.

Langland, W., *Piers Plowman*, C Text, ed. Derek Pearsall (York Medieval Texts), Arnold, London, 1978.

Ludus Coventriae, ed. K. S. Block, E.E.T.S. e.s. 120, 1922.

Lydgate, J., *Siege of Thebes*, ed. A. Erdmann and E. Ekwall, E.E.T.S. e.s. 108 and 125, 1911 and 1930.

Macro Plays, ed. Mark Eccles, E.E.T.S. o.s. 262, 1969.

Malory, T., *Works*, ed. E. Vinaver (Oxford Standard Authors), 2nd edn., Oxford University Press, Oxford, 1971.

Mannyng, R., *Handlyng Synne*, ed. F. J. Furnivall, E.E.T.S. o.s. 119 and 123, 1901 and 1903.

N Town Cycle, see *Ludus Coventriae*.

Owl and the Nightingale, ed. E. G. Stanley (Nelson's Medieval and Renaissance Library), Nelson, London, 1960.

Patience, ed. J. J. Anderson, Manchester University Press, Manchester, 1969.

Pearl, ed. E. V. Gordon, Clarendon Press, Oxford, 1953.

Peterborough Chronicle, ed. C. Clark, Oxford University Press, Oxford, 1958.

Purity, see *Cleanness*.

St Erkenwald, ed. Clifford Peterson, University of Pennsylvania Press, 1977.

Sir Beves of Hamtoun, ed. E. Kölbing, E.E.T.S. e.s. 46, 48 and 65, 1885, 1886 and 1894.

Sir Gawain and the Green Knight, ed. J. R. R. Tolkein and E. V. Gordon, 2nd edn., revised N. Davis, Clarendon Press, Oxford, 1967.

Sir Orfeo, ed. A. J. Bliss, 2nd edn., Clarendon Press, Oxford, 1966.

Towneley Plays, ed. G. England and A. W. Pollard, E.E.T.S. e.s. 71, 1897.

Winner and Waster, ed. I. Gollancz, Oxford University Press, Oxford, 1921 (reissued Brewer, Cambridge, 1974).

York Plays, ed. Lucy Toulmin Smith, Clarendon Press, Oxford, 1885.

Ywain and Gawain, ed. A. B. Friedman and N. T. Harrington, E.E.T.S. o.s. 254, 1964.

Studies (excluding studies of individual authors)

Auerbach, E., *Mimesis: The Representation of Reality in Western Literature*, trans. W. R. Trask, Doubleday, New York, 1957.

Baugh, A. C., and Malone, Kemp, *The Middle Ages* (*A Literary History of England*, Vol. I), 2nd edn., Routledge, London, 1967.

Blake, N. F., *The English Language in Medieval Literature*, Methuen, London, 1979.

Burrow, J. A., *Ricardian Poetry*, Routledge, London, 1971.

Chaytor, H. J., *From Script to Print: An Introduction to Medieval Literature*, Cambridge University Press, Cambridge, 1945.

Clanchy, M. T., *From Memory to Written Record: England 1066–1307*, Arnold, London, 1979.

Curtius, E. R., *European Literature and the Latin Middle Ages*, trans. W. R. Trask, Routledge, London, 1953.

Dronke, P., *The Medieval Lyric*, Hutchinson, London, 1968.

Eisenstein, E., *The Printing Press as an Agent of Change*, Cambridge University Press, Cambridge, 1979.

Everett, D., *Essays on Middle English Literature*, ed. P. M. Kean, Oxford University Press, Oxford, 1955.

Faral, E. (ed.), *Les Arts Poétiques du XIIe et du XIIIe Siècle* (Bibliothèque de l'École des Hautes Études, No. 238), Champion, Paris, 1924.

Goldschmidt, E. P., *Medieval Texts and their First Appearance in Print* (Supplement to the Bibliographical Society's Transactions, No. 16), Bibliographical Society, London, 1943.

Gradon, P., *Form and Style in Early English Literature*, Methuen, London, 1971.

Gray, D., *Themes and Images in the Medieval English Religious Lyric*, Routledge, London, 1972.

Greene, R. L., *The Early English Carols*, 2nd edn., Clarendon Press, Oxford, 1977.

Ker, W. P., *Epic and Romance: Essays on Medieval Literature*, London, 1897 (reissued Dover, New York, 1957).

Kolve, V. A., *The Play Called Corpus Christi*, Stanford University Press, Stanford, California, 1966.

Lewis, C. S., *The Allegory of Love: A Study of Medieval Tradition*, Oxford University Press, Oxford, 1936.

Lewis, C. S., *The Discarded Image: An Introduction to Medieval and Renaissance Literature*, Cambridge University Press, Cambridge, 1964.

Loomis, R. S. (ed.), *Arthurian Literature in the Middle Ages*, Clarendon Press, Oxford, 1959.

Mathew, G., *The Court of Richard II*, Murray, London, 1968.

Mehl, D., *The Middle English Romances of the Thirteenth and Fourteenth Centuries*, Routledge, London, 1968.

Morris, Colin, *The Discovery of the Individual 1050–1200*, S.P.C.K., London, 1972.

Nykrog, P., *Les Fabliaux*, Munksgaard, Copenhagen, 1957.

Owst, G. R., *Literature and Pulpit in Medieval England*, Cambridge University Press, Cambridge, 1933 (reissued Blackwell, Oxford, 1961).

Pearsall, D., *Old English and Middle English Poetry* (*Routledge History of English Poetry*, Vol. I), Routledge, London, 1977.

Preminger, A. S., Hardison, O. B., and Kerrane, K., *Classical and Medieval Literary Criticism: Translations and Interpretations*, Ungar, New York, 1974.

Robertson, D. W., *A Preface to Chaucer*, Princeton University Press, Princeton, 1962.

Southern, R. W., *The Making of the Middle Ages*, Hutchinson, London, 1953.

Spearing, A. C., *Criticism and Medieval Poetry*, 2nd edn., Arnold, London, 1972.

Stevens, John, *Medieval Romance: Themes and Approaches*, Hutchinson, London, 1973.

Stevens, John, *Music and Poetry in the Early Tudor Court*, Methuen, London, 1961 (reissued Cambridge University Press, Cambridge, 1979).

Turville-Petre, T., *The Alliterative Revival*, Brewer, Cambridge, 1977.

Tuve, R., *Allegorical Imagery: Some Mediaeval Books and their Posterity*, Princeton University Press, Princeton, 1966.

Vinaver, E., *The Rise of Romance*, Clarendon Press, Oxford, 1971.

Welter, J-T., *L'Exemplum dans la Littérature Religieuse et Didactique du Moyen Age*, Guitard, Paris, 1927.

Wilson, R. M., *The Lost Literature of Medieval England*, 2nd edn., Methuen, London, 1970.

Woolf, R., *The English Mystery Plays*, Routledge, London, 1972.

Woolf, R., *The English Religious Lyric in the Middle Ages*, Clarendon Press, Oxford, 1968.

Index

OXFORD

MORE OXFORD PAPERBACKS

Details of a selection of other books follow. A complete list of Oxford Paperbacks, including The World's Classics, Twentieth-Century Classics, OPUS, Past Masters, Oxford Authors, Oxford Shakespeare, and Oxford Paperback Reference, is available in the UK from the General Publicity Department, Oxford University Press (JN), Walton Street, Oxford OX2 6DP.

In the USA, complete lists are available from the Paperbacks Marketing Manager, Oxford University Press, 200 Madison Avenue, New York, NY 10016.

Oxford Paperbacks are available from all good bookshops. In case of difficulty, customers in the UK can order direct from Oxford University Press Bookshop, 116 High Street, Oxford, Freepost, OX1 4BR, enclosing full payment. Please add 10 per cent of published price for postage and packing.

THE OXFORD BOOK OF LATE MEDIEVAL VERSE AND PROSE

Edited by Douglas Gray

In this illuminating anthology the late medieval period—from the death of Chaucer to the early years of Henry VIII's reign—emerges as an age of great literary achievement. The works of familiar authors such as Malory, Henryson, Skelton, and More are well-represented, along with well-known styles including songs and lyrics, ballads and romances. The Testament of Cresseid, Mankind, and Everyman are given in full, and the anthology also includes some works never before published.

'The range of texts is astonishing . . . Gray writes with all the sharp and authoritative abservation of a C. S. Lewis.' *Times Literary Supplement*

THE ALLEGORY OF LOVE

Study in Medieval Tradition

C. S. Lewis

First published in 1936, this classic study in medieval tradition traces the rise of the sentiment called 'Courtly Love' and of the allegorical method from eleventh-century Languedoc to sixteenth-century England. C. S. Lewis devotes considerable attention to *The Romance of the Rose* and *The Faerie Queene*, and to such poets as Chaucer, Gower, and Thomas Usk.

'a truly great work' *Observer*

'scholarly fascinating, and original' *Times Literary Supplement*